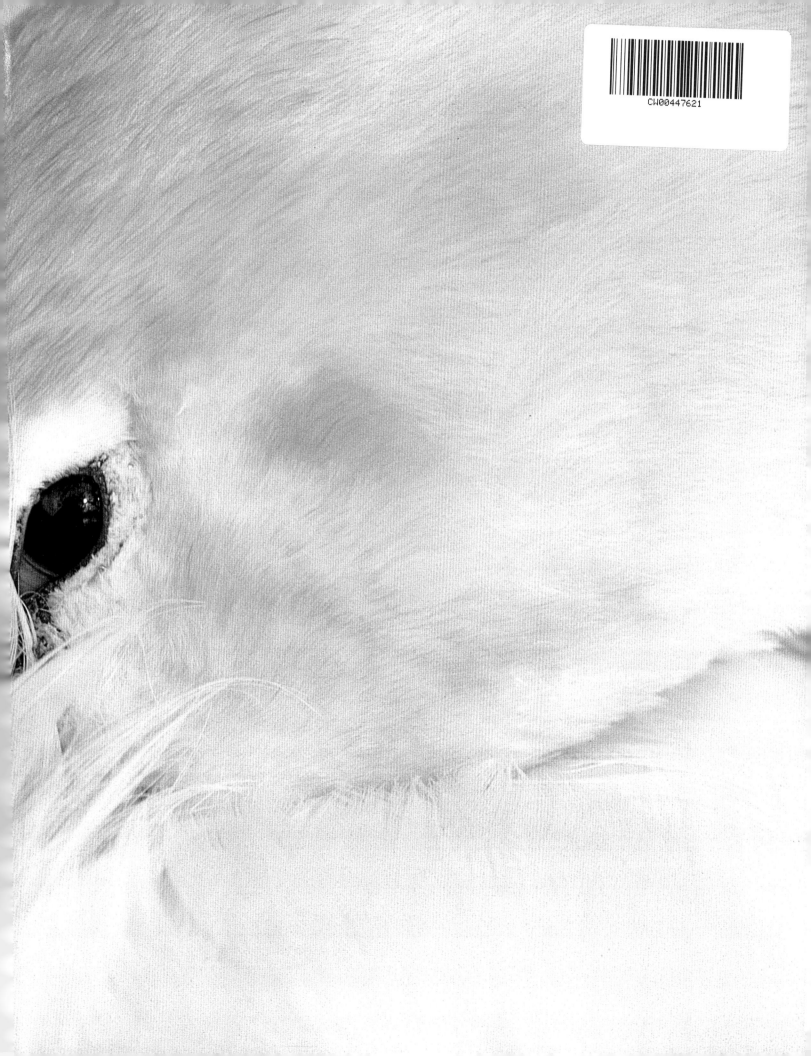

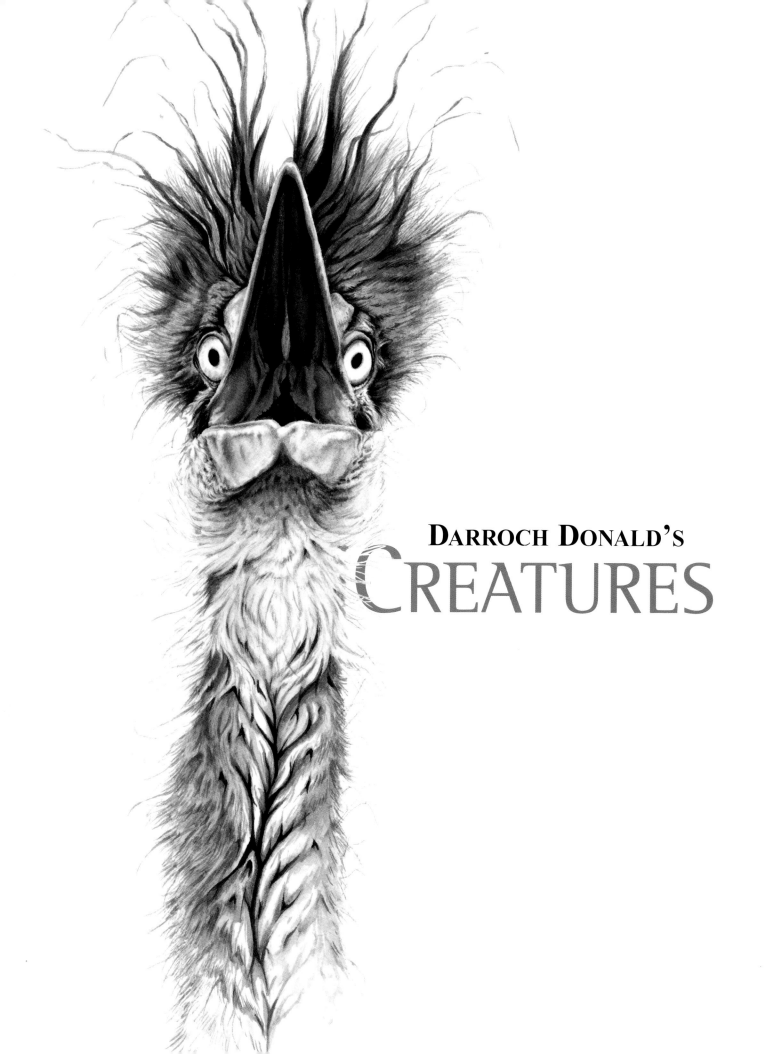

DARROCH DONALD'S
CREATURES

DARROCH DONALD'S
CREATURES

Hodder & Stoughton

Acknowledgements

I would like to thank the following in particular for their help and encouragement over the years and the contribution they have made in the realisation of a dream – this book.

As a boy, when wildlife rescue was a hobby:

Veterinarian David More and vet nurse Mij Peacock; Robin and Pam Waterston; ornithologist Ian Cumming; wildlife rehabilitators Alan and Jean Bryant.

Later on in life, when the hobby became my occupation:

Middlebank Animal Welfare Centre staff Sandra Hogben and Gill Wood; volunteers Shirley Jenkins, Jim Taylor, Callum McGregor, Peter McLeod, John Dupuy, Ian and Janice Bork, Alistair Marcol, Alan Robinson and the many others who played and continue to play such a vital role.

Veterinarians Joe Ryan, Aileen Calder and staff; Tim Thomas of the RSPCA; Les Peters and Bill Brown of the *Dundee Courier*; Neil Pumford, Rod and Elaine Lambert; Sea Mammals Research Unit.

In New Zealand where my occupation became my dream:

Piers Hayman; Wildlife Veterinarian Wayne Boardman; Barbara Nielsen for her interest, encouragement and invaluable assistance, and the team at Hodder Moa Beckett.

A special thanks to Editorial Consultant Kirsten Warner for her help and guidance in the art of writing.

Also a big thanks to my mother, Grace, and partner, Julia, who not only support and encourage me but are always there when I have experienced the "wild" in life and have found myself in need of rescue and rehabilitation.

Note

All the stories in this book are based on fact. The author wishes to emphasise, however, that some aspects of the stories are representational and the creatures may be composites of a number of individuals.

Editorial Consultant

Helping shape these stories was Kirsten Warner, who has an extensive background in journalism, writing and television, working for the *Auckland Star* and as a feature writer for the *NZ Herald*. She was runner-up in the 1994 *Sunday Star Times* short story competition, and winner of the 1996 Rotorua Community Arts Council short story competition. Kirsten teaches writing to working journalists and currently freelances for a number of magazines and newspapers in New Zealand and overseas.

For Grace

The beauty and genius of a work of art

may be reconceived,

though its first material expression

be destroyed;

a vanished harmony may yet again

inspire the composer;

but when the last individual

of a race of living things

breathes no more,

another heaven and another earth

must pass

before such a one can be again.

William Beebe (1877–1962)
American naturalist and explorer

Darroch Donald's
Creatures

CONTENTS

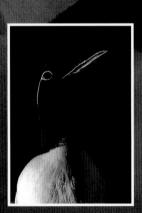

INTRODUCTION

INROADS

EXPLAINING TO OTHERS WHY I WORK IN WILDLIFE RESCUE HAS ALWAYS BEEN DIFFICULT. IT HAS TAKEN A LONG TIME TO ACCEPT THAT MY NATURAL PASSION FOR WILDLIFE AND THE ROADS I TRAVEL EXPLORING THIS PASSION ARE CONSIDERED UNUSUAL BY MOST PEOPLE.

It seems that my love and respect for other creatures and the way I demonstrate this makes me quite a rare creature myself. Even my closest friends, who understand my work and who have supported me through life's ups and downs, will sometimes ask in despair or exasperation why I don't get a proper job.

The journey has proved to be hard and lonely as well as exciting and rewarding, but it has never been dull. It is a journey that I can be proud of and it has always provided me with a clear direction.

My mother still describes me as a great one for the bugs. My father summed up my early interest in wildlife with the story about the first day he took me to play golf. It was, according to my father, a somewhat frustrating affair, because every time I lost my ball he would lose me. The only clue to my whereabouts was the abandoned golf bag next to the undergrowth, and some time later I would innocently emerge with a caterpillar and a satisfied smile.

A fledgling dunnock with big aspirations.

Although proudly of Scots blood, I was born in Leeds and spent the first seven years of my life in the town of Ilkely in Yorkshire. Mine was a happy and secure childhood and I was able to satisfy the early rumblings of a fascination for wildlife with collections of frog spawn and an admirable range of creepy crawlies or anything else I could catch.

I do recall one incident in those early years that could have curtailed my interest in wildlife. I did not, at that time, understand that the creepy crawlies in question might not always be as happy as I was about their enforced captivity, and when I found a wasps' nest I decided the entire colony would make a great addition to my collection. One hundred and fifty stings later I had learnt the hard way that wildlife can be truly wild, and to this day I am a little wary of wasps and remain allergic to them.

My secure world was shattered and my wildlife collection disbanded when I was seven years old and my mother, Grace, separated from my father, Bill. She, my brother, Ghill, and I moved to the Lake District. It proved a difficult time for all of us, but I found comfort and solace on my own by the river, which was proving to be the source of a new and even more exciting wildlife collection.

St Andrews from West Sands – a beach which was imprinted by my youthful footsteps almost daily. On this particular day, unusually, everything was blanketed with snow.

In pride of place amongst the boxes and jars in the basement lived my collection of newts. To me they looked like miniature dinosaurs and were accorded due respect. I had acquired an aquarium where my crayfish served time. The biggest was perhaps only eight centimetres long but, as far as I was concerned, it was huge. My mother delivered strict instructions that whatever lived in the jars downstairs in the basement was not allowed to come upstairs, especially under its own steam. Fortunately, I was learning that wildlife is wild and best left that way and gradually I began to spend more hours observing by the river than down in the basement.

After a year my mother decided we should move on and she headed home to Scotland, where she had secured a job in a bookshop in the east coast town of St Andrews in the county of Fife. I looked forward with great excitement to living by the sea and had visions of the most monumental wildlife collection.

The day we arrived that collection almost began immediately. On a road junction on the outskirts of St Andrews I spotted a bird lying in the road and let out a yelp. If only to avoid an accident, my mother stopped the car. I gathered up the pathetic-looking sparrow and made it comfortable in a

The one-winged mallard duck, christened, of course, Donald. With my surname, could it have been named anything else?

Opposite: When I was a teenage wildlife rehabilitator, the ducks in our family bathtub were the real thing not rubber. Eider ducks, in this case a female, were common among my first patients.

box of tissues. It was my first wildlife rescue and my first injured bird, the first of many and the start of a new direction. Before we arrived at our new address it had died.

The upset was short-lived, and before the unpacking had started I headed for the beach merely metres away. I stood looking at the waves in awe. I think Mum anticipated my excitement. Finding me knee-deep in a rock pool, she dragged me home and showed me the garden shed – the place where my inevitable new wildlife collection would be housed. I immersed myself in a new and wonderful world.

What I saw, did and learnt along those five kilometres of Scottish coastline was to shape the rest of my life. Now that I was settled in a new school and all of us were a lot happier, I spent all my spare time on the beach. For extra pocket money I cleaned the bookshop where my mother worked. After it was closed I would abandon the vacuum cleaner and sit well into the long winter evenings engrossed in wildlife books.

Already quite adept at bird identification, it wasn't long before I became something of a local expert. My friends and their parents would often describe some creature they had spotted and ask me for its proper name.

It was perhaps inevitable that I would begin to encounter sick or injured birds, and it was an entirely natural thing for me to try to take them into care. Unfortunately, I did not anticipate my mother's reaction when I took my first patient home. Looking back I can see that perhaps the bath was not the best place to house an eider duck with diarrhoea.

Once the initial shock had abated, my mother gradually accepted my determination to become the local animal search and rescue. Provided my patients were housed outside, she accepted, although sometimes a little uneasily, that my wildlife collection was quickly developing into a wildlife hospital.

The next inevitable step was towards the local veterinary surgery, where, amongst assorted dogs, cats and strange looks, I booked in the contents of a cardboard box under the name "Donald, injured duck!".

It was the beginning of a close and mutually beneficial relationship with the practice and its staff. They had someone to take care of any injured wildlife that came in, and in return for free treatment I turned from cleaning the local bookshop to cleaning the veterinary surgery, with the added responsibilities of Saturday receptionist and, of course, general dogsbody.

Our early attempts with these first casualties was an important period of learning, most often through trial and error. Regardless of facilities, knowledge or professionalism, successes in wildlife rehabilitation are a bonus. Much of the time, trying to bring them back to full health was as

difficult as climbing mountains with clogs on. Disappointment became a familiar feeling.

Before long the general public was arriving on our family doorstep with assorted creatures for me to nurse. Donald, the one-winged duck, was living in a pen on the roof, and the bath had been repeatedly hijacked in the cause of some water creature or other, so it was understandable that my mother's patience was beginning to wane. When she discovered another duck hidden in the airing cupboard, this time with extraordinary bowel problems, a law reform bill was formally and sternly passed. Wildlife lived outside and would stay outside.

Luckily a friend moved into a nearby property that had an old aviary in the garden, and I was invited to house my creatures there. Tranquillity returned to the domestic front. I set about repairing the aviary and, before long, although not the prettiest aviary around it was at least secure and ready for its first tenant. On the day of the great aviary opening I went out onto the roof to take Donald to his new lodgings and found the duck had disappeared.

I searched the roof and adjoining gardens and, somewhat distraught, began to question the owners of the surrounding properties, one of which was a butcher's shop.

"What's it to be laddie?" said the rotund, red-faced butcher.

"Got any duck?" I said.

"Well, funny you should say that. Don't usually have duck but I found one in the garden yesterday. Had one wing and a funny walk. Thought I was seeing things," he said.

"So where is it now?" I said, expecting the worst.

"A one-wing duck's as much use as an ashtray on a motorbike, in'it?" he said laughing. "I rung its neck, laddie, gave it to the dog."

I stood aghast and, before the tears rimmed my eyes, I left the shop. I planned the demise of the rotund, red-faced murderer for months, but the nearest I came to revenge was the systematic kidnapping and execution of his garden gnome collection.

In my teens I belonged to the local bird club and spent a lot of time watching and identifying birds, but was beginning to pursue the more conventional teenage pastimes. School work took priority over rescuing injured wildlife, and so did the decision about what I wanted to do with my future.

I set my sights on an art college in Wales, which was unique in offering a three-year diploma in wildlife illustration, and took a year off from school to compile a portfolio for the interview. I began to record with a pencil and on film the creatures I encountered.

From an early age I began to record the creatures I encountered in pencil and on film. This captive kestrel belonged to a local falconer.

In February 1983, armed with my portfolio and an overnight bag, I headed south to Wales for the interview. In the rain and the darkness I climbed out of the train onto a deserted Carmarthen platform, booked myself into the nearest bed and breakfast, and hid in my room till morning. In daylight Carmarthen did not seem so bad, and with determined gait I headed for the art college. Within half an hour I was spilling ten-pence coins all over a phone box as I called my mother with the good news: I had been accepted into the second year due to the standard of my portfolio.

I have some very fond memories of art college and Wales. It provided an important grounding in various artistic disciplines and, more than anything else, taught me about other human beings. I was able to maintain my close contact with wildlife and wildlife rehabilitation through an association with the New Quay Bird Hospital and its founders, Jean and Alan Bryant. They operated a small, private unit at their home near a picturesque fishing village in the county of Dyfed, just a bus ride from the art college and Carmarthen.

I had first made contact with the Bryants as a boy after reading about their work in a magazine. I had been cleaning up my hospital ward (my wooden shed) one afternoon and, while lining a wildlife holding box with newspaper, I stopped to flick through a colour supplement. My eyes nearly popped from their sockets when I spotted a photo of a couple holding a swan in their arms. Eagerly I read the accompanying article about their efforts in saving wildlife, including oiled birds.

Within minutes a letter with the heading "Help" was dropped in the mail box and was soon winging its way to the Bryants. A week and another dead oiled bird later I got a reply that contained pages full of information, techniques and above all some solid and positive encouragement.

A page from my first patient log book started when I was 13.

It was the first of many such letters and, although my lack of facilities did not improve my mortality figures, these letters did provide things equally important – hope and encouragement for the future, and a valuable and influential relationship.

So as soon as I could put a weekend aside I jumped on the bus and headed for New Quay. As we passed through a network of small country roads bordered by hedgerows and stone walls the number of passengers dwindled, and I climbed from an empty bus at a cross roads next to the aptly named Cross Inn Public House. I headed up what I assumed was the Bryants' driveway, descended into a wooded glade and was entranced by the special atmosphere surrounding the sprawling, Swiss Family Robinson sort of house and the out-buildings with their familiar smell of wildlife.

Jean came to the door. "Darroch?" she said with a huge smile. "Quick, you're just in time for a seal feed. Alan had to pop out so can you give me

a hand?" It was all the introduction we needed. Jean struggled into a minute pair of wellies, while I fought with a pair of oversized waders and followed her to a small building beyond the house. By the time we got there I had received an almost complete case history of Ripple, the seal pup.

I had not been there ten minutes and already I was handling wildlife. I felt entirely at home.

I stayed the weekend, forgetting all about the outside world and engrossed in the hospital and its patients. Alan smoked a briar pipe like Sherlock Holmes, which scented the house with the rich smell of tobacco, and he had a sense of humour that would reduce me to tears. Jean was a veritable powerhouse of a woman. The Bryant menagerie held a very special magic. Of all the people I have encountered in the business of wildlife rescue and rehabilitation the Bryants remain the most genuine and kind. My regular visits provided the continuation of my contact with wildlife, a venue to practise my art and strengthen my interest and knowledge of wildlife rehabilitation.

In June 1986, with a diploma in wildlife illustration and my first exhibition under my belt, and a lot less naive about life in general, I returned once more to Scotland and my old coastal haunts.

All that experience was great, but where on earth could I now go to earn a living using it? I had visions of my wildlife involvement becoming a strictly weekend love affair and, terrified at the prospect, I put most of my time into bird watching and very little into seeking employment. Four

Opposite and left: In my early years, a gannet was a large and dangerous patient which featured in my log book (previous page).

The new Oiled Bird Cleaning Centre at Middlebank Farm near Dunfermline shortly after opening in November 1986. A first for Scotland and my new found *raison d'être*.

months passed and, prompted by guilt and boredom, I finally found myself a job with the local council as a graphic artist, creating displays at an interpretive countryside centre in a country park on the outskirts of town. At least I was perhaps heading in the right direction.

My lucky break came one morning in the autumn of 1986. I have never been a great one for reading the daily newspaper. If and when I did it was usually a case of scanning the headlines for anything concerning wildlife, which was most often brief and bad news. But that morning I read a small headline that made me literally jump out of my seat with excitement. The Scottish Society for the Prevention of Cruelty to Animals (SSPCA) was to open Scotland's first oiled bird cleaning centre near the town of Dunfermline, not far from Edinburgh.

It was hoped to duplicate the success of a similar centre run by the RSPCA, which had been operating for the past 14 years at Taunton in England. I recalled the days as a boy when the local SSPCA inspector would bring me sick and injured birds, so I was aware of the society's work and, more importantly, its predicament. Most people didn't realise that the English and the Scottish societies, both about 150 years old, were separate organisations. The Scottish society, being smaller, had no purpose-built wildlife facilities, but it was expected to fulfil the same obligations as the English society.

By the time I'd finished reading and rereading those few column inches, the dog had finished my breakfast and was heading out the door. The word "Staff" spinning round my head propelled me towards the telephone. Head office gave me the number of Sandra Hogben, a wildlife rehabilitator living near Dunfermline. She had been rescuing oiled birds and keeping them in makeshift facilities at home, and was, by all accounts, the driving force behind the project. I phoned Sandra and eagerly told her of my experience and my desire to be part of the new Scottish project. Although there were no jobs available she was keen to get me involved, and I immediately put my name down on her volunteer list.

We made an appointment to meet at Middlebank Farmstead, the site of the proposed oiled bird cleaning centre, to talk further and let me see the building work nearing completion. The inspector for south-west Fife would live in the farmhouse, and new barns, pools, drying rooms, reception room, kitchen, office and boat storage barn were being built around it.

The society recognised the urgent need to be prepared to deal with a coastal oil spill. Dunfermline was two minutes from the motorway, and 20 minutes to SSPCA headquarters in Edinburgh, and it was relatively cheap to buy a suitable property there. But, more importantly, it was ideally situated on the Forth of Firth, a place very likely to experience an oil spill because of the millions of tons of crude oil travelling through the Forth by supertanker to the Grangemouth oil refinery. About eight kilometres from the centre, below the famous Forth rail bridge, was the Hound Point pumping station, where tankers unloaded. With a new pipeline coming down from the north, there was even more risk of an environmental disaster.

(Once established, the centre catered for the whole of Scotland and also received birds from spills in Northern Ireland over the years.)

I had found the road I was looking for. Already Sandra had non-oiled creatures filling rooms in which the paint was still drying, and someone had to be there all day and every day to care for them. To the general public there was no difference between oiled and non-oiled wildlife, and I knew that the small farmstead on the outskirts of Dunfermline would, by accident or design, soon become a complete wildlife rehabilitation centre. I decided that if the SSPCA were not already aware of that they should be told and I set about writing a detailed letter to the chief executive about my vision and how I could help them develop it. It was perhaps a little pushy, but by now I was a man with a mission.

I eagerly awaited a response from the chief executive. When it arrived it was polite but wary, and he was adamant that the centre would deal only with oiled birds. I accepted the response, but when it came to wildlife rehabilitation I was perhaps a little wiser so I decided to remain closely involved and quietly let events take their course.

Just as the beaches of St Andrews had been when I was a child,

Middlebank three years after opening, showing the new aviary and enclosures. Just as I had predicted, it was growing at a phenomenal rate.

Middlebank now became my *raison d'être*. My part-time work was now an encumbrance. I spent as much time as I could helping at the centre and sketching its first patients, and for the first year I travelled the 145-kilometre round trip in my mother's car, or by bus or train, every weekend or two and stayed over for three or four days. I look back on those first brief encounters with a special fondness, perhaps simply because at that stage I could still afford so much time alone with each of those animals.

In March 1987, while I was still a volunteer, Middlebank dealt with its first major oil spill, and in September that year I formally took up the position of assistant manager at what is now known as the SSPCA Middlebank Animal Welfare Centre. By Christmas I had bought a miniature bachelor flat in Limekilns, the picturesque village where Sandra and her husband lived.

I had been spoiled at St Andrews, where tourists often stopped and admired our historic fisherman's cottage, and I was shocked by the grim poverty and the housing estates of Dunfermline. Although an ancient town, it had suffered the same fate as the rest of industrialised southern Scotland when coal mining, ship building and other industries closed down and jobs were lost. Limekilns was prettier and more like home, although I ended up spending very little time there. I usually retreated to my flat exhausted, washed, threw together a makeshift meal and slept.

It was at times lonely and solitary work for a young man, and I was constantly disappointed that other people found it so unusual.

"So what do you do then?" they'd ask.

"Clean oiled birds," I'd reply, anticipating the response.

"You what? Clean oiled bugs?"

Oh dear, there's that look again. "No . . . birds," I'd say.

I was 21 when I first started at Middlebank as a volunteer and 22 when I became assistant manager. My friends were still finishing university at Edinburgh, and I managed to maintain a hectic social life with them, as well as going away on golfing weekends and walking trips in the highlands with friends or on my own with the family dog.

Caring for wildlife was on a 24-hour basis, and you had to be flexible with your time keeping. Often that meant coming in for the first feed at 8am, feeding and cleaning throughout the day, going home for a bite to eat in the early evening and then returning for the last feed at 11pm. At times the work was physically and emotionally draining. I became exhausted, and in the middle of my time at Middlebank, after a disastrous love affair, I was told to take three months' leave to recover.

I loved the work, and there was not exactly a surfeit of other jobs for wildlife rehabilitators and artists, so, although the job had definite drawbacks and I sometimes clashed with the rather conservative SSPCA hierarchy, I stuck it out for another couple of years. I must have been at times gloomy and difficult to deal with. I was recovering from my broken heart and finding people much harder to accept and deal with than animals.

During my four years at the centre we dealt with over six thousand wild creatures. My work saw me spending Christmas Days force feeding seal pups; rescuing seal pups from bath tubs, busy high streets and even public telephone boxes; extracting a shag from under a Navy submarine in dry dock; chasing swans around ponds in a rubber inflatable; and flying over the oil-devastated coast of the Persian Gulf with the US Marines surveying the environmental devastation after the Gulf War.

This book is not the story of Middlebank. It is not about me or other people who worked there. Neither is it meant as a guide to caring for wildlife. It is a collection of stories of some of the creatures I encountered and who touched my heart and my life, seen through the eyes of an artist and a photographer.

During the four years I spent at Middlebank I built up a store of stories about its patients, some of whom stand out as complete and identifiable characters – like Bottle, the heron chick with the outrageously quirky

Centre manager Sandra Hogben with four abandoned swan cygnets. We had our hands full at Middlebank caring for an assortment of waifs, strays and injuries – quite literally in this instance.

character. Bottle was unforgettable, and I spent many hours photographing and drawing him. Because of the pressures of time, I was simply unable to follow all the other creatures, so, for the purposes of this book, the photographs and stories are representative of the incidents and anecdotes I remember.

Wildlife rehabilitation is a way of life for me, so I was grateful to be able to follow my heart. But the work was demanding, stressful, financially unrewarding and at times dreadfully disappointing. There was, I remember, only one day in my four years at Middlebank when we had no creature in residence. I decided I had to find another way to help wildlife and I had no doubt how I wanted to do that. I turned to my camera and my pencils and began again to record my wildlife encounters. It was then that the idea for this book was conceived.

On the evolutionary scale we are children compared to most of the creatures we share this earth with. But, like delinquent children, we act without guidance and destroy without thought, and seemingly without repercussion. We have a choice, yet it is a choice we ignore or are blind to. And if and when we take a fall, where and to whom can we run? Mother nature?

With these thoughts in mind, the aim of this book is simple. Through these stories and photographs I hope you will see, as I do, the often thoughtless and unintentional ways in which we are endangering wildlife, and will learn something about what can be done to offer them the protection and respect they so richly deserve. I wish to share their lives with you in the hope that you realise, if you haven't already, that we share our lives with them.

Opposite: One of the highlights of my career in wildlife rescue – releasing cleaned birds with the US Marines during the Persian Gulf eco-disaster.

Middlebank could not have functioned, much less thrived, without committed volunteers (as I was initially). I built up a good rapport with two of our valued workers, Shirley Jenkins and Jim Taylor, reclining with centre mascot Willoughby (I'm at the rear).

BACARDI

A SEAL PUP ON THE ROCKS

IT WAS A ROUGH START TO THE MORNING. I GRABBED THE PHONE AND HEARD THE VOICE OF MIJ PEACOCK, THE LOCAL VETERINARY SURGERY NURSE: "DID I WAKE YOU UP, YOU LAZY BUGGER . . . IT'S ALL RIGHT FOR SOME, HAVEN'T YOU FOUND A JOB YET?"

I'd been out with the lads the night before in Edinburgh, and it had been a long and varied evening. My closest friends from St Andrews and school days were still at university and, as students are apt to do, played as hard as they worked. Although I'd finished my training and had launched myself into what I passionately hoped would be a career in wildlife rescue, I was still only 21 and had a lot of youthful business to attend to.

"Hmm . . . Good morning Mij, yes to the first question. As for other question, I told you there's only one job I'm after, and that's as an assistant at the oiled bird centre. You know that."

"Oh, aye," she said, "how is the centre? We never see you any more. We miss the odd duck in the surgery, you know, and the new vet said I should put your picture up on our lost and found window but I didn't want to scare the customers."

I chuckled. I liked Mij; she was in her mid-thirties, a lot of fun and down to earth, and we got along well. She had been the long-suffering nurse at

Bacardi – lurking just behind those big appealing eyes was a young lady with attitude.

the veterinary surgery of Orr, Duff and Howat's as long as I'd been bringing them waifs and strays, and she was dedicated to animals. If she was calling me, it had to be about something wild and homeless. "Very funny," I said. "So what's up?"

"Selkie. Now that's a nickname for a seal pup, isn't it?"

"Aye . . . grey seal pup . . . still with its white coat, once said to harbour the souls of dead sailors, and they wail better than any human baby. Why?" I was definitely interested.

"Good," she said, "at least I got that right. Well, you'd better get yourself down to St Monance. There's one in trouble on the beach, by the church."

"You're joking," I said, thinking fast. "Right . . . brilliant, I mean. Damn it . . . transport, a car. Er . . . who phoned you?"

"A Mrs McCormick, a minute ago, and her kids have been trying to feed it crisps."

"Oh, my Lord," I said. "Quick, for goodness' sake, phone her back and tell her to grab the kids right now . . . it'll take their fingers off. And tell her I'll be there as soon as possible . . . . Oh, and tell her to keep people away from it, herself included. I'll speak to you later. By the church you said?"

"Aye . . . but what about your fingers . . . ?" But by the time she had said it I had hung up and was dialling a friend to arrange some transport.

My long-suffering friend Harry McIlvenny, who was studying to be a doctor, was home from Edinburgh for the weekend. But he had been duped into many a quest before and was rather canny about getting roped in again.

"Harry . . . listen, it's Darroch here," I said. "Listen, am I absolutely right in thinking you would love to meet a Miss McCormick?"

"Really?" said Harry. "Miss McCormick, eh? You're sure it's definitely Miss?"

"Yep."

"Well . . . yes, okay, definitely. Yes . . . lead me to her."

"Brilliant. Just get yourself and the car round here now. She lives down the road."

It didn't take long for Harry to drive around. Soon we were heading at high speed towards the small fishing village of St Monance, 25 kilometres away on the shores of the Firth of Forth, while Harry looked with concern at the odometer. "Down the bloody road," he muttered. "This'd better be worth it, Darroch. Last time I went on one of your wild goose chases I ended up stuck up to my knees in the middle of the estuary mud flats with the tide coming in."

Above and opposite: With their white pre-weaner coat, grey seal pups, or "selkies", as they are called in Scotland, looked wonderfully cute and cuddly – but in reality, when it came to human contact, they were more like sharks in fur coats.

"Oh aye . . . I remember that," I said giggling. "We were after that bird, weren't we?" When it came to a wildlife mission, I was without remorse.

"Well, Sunshine," he stared me straight in the eye, "the only bird I meet today had better be Miss McCormick, okay?"

"Absolutely," I replied, trying to hide a smile.

As we drew up at the church and approached a petite older lady (by older I mean older than 21) standing at the church gates, I could see Harry's face gradually elongating. The lady looked very concerned and held a child's hand tightly in cach of hers.

"Ah, you must be Miss McCormick," I said.

"No . . . it's Mrs, Irene actually, and these are my sons, John and Toby. Toby's been crying; the seal turned on him. For a wee thing that looks like death, it's got some fight in it."

She pointed towards the beach and, after grabbing a blanket and some thick gloves I'd hastily put in the boot, we headed in the general direction.

Once home to a colony of monks, the Isle of May, at the mouth of the Firth of Forth, is now void of human habitation and left as it should be – protected home to precious colonies of seabirds and seals.

I negotiated the slippery rocks with an action that must have looked more like the highland fling than walking, paused to get my bearings and spotted the seal pup a short distance away.

As I approached she raised her weary head a few centimetres in my direction. With a huge effort she turned and wailed, spitting steam and wet, blood-stained sand from her mouth. She was in a terrible state. She had old and new wounds, festering or trickling with blood; the flap of flesh that was the remains of her umbilicus was ripped and pecked to tatters, and one eye was so swollen I was not sure if it was still there.

"You poor devil," I whispered, moving in to take a closer look. Even in such a state, there was something infinitely appealing about a seal pup and I was tempted to hold out my bare hand to touch her, but knew better. Without warning she exploded in anger and swung her shivering body around towards me, hissing with defiance. But the effort was too much and she fell into semi-consciousness.

Quickly I gloved up, placed the towel over her entire body and, grabbing the back of her neck first, gathered her up in to my arms. By the time I had negotiated the slippery rocks back on to the sand Harry and the minister from the church were standing by Irene's side.

"It must have come from May Isle," said the minister. "I thought it was a child calling out just now," he said, placing his hand gently on Toby's head. "Got a real fright."

"Aye, well . . . they're usually born out with the colony, although occasionally it's too crowded over there and you find adults giving birth on mainland beaches. As a rule you should leave the pups alone. They've usually been abandoned only recently and they have to find their own way; or, if they're still suckling, Mum is usually around somewhere. But this one's in a terrible state, isn't it? I'll do what I can." I placed the seal pup in the back of the car, where it sat precariously. "Thanks for calling the vet, Irene."

"God bless," said the minister.

For a while we drove in deep impenetrable silence, save for the irregular breathing of my new charge. "Harry . . . I . . . ."

"Say nothing. Just do not say anything," said Harry.

The car filled with the pungent smell of seaweed and that definite smell of seal. I remembered it from my first close encounter in Wales. It was certainly unique and was an odour that would quite soon become almost part of me. But Harry was not impressed. "Where now?" he barked.

I thought I had better sound as if I really knew where we were going with it and, what's more, was entirely confident, but in reality my mind was racing. This was one patient even my mother would not put up with in the bath. It was clearly beyond the realms of decency to ask Harry to drive all the way to the oiled bird centre at Middlebank, and, besides, the centre had not yet dealt with any seals. But who was I trying to kid? Aside from the cleaning of a few pens and helping with some feeding at the Bryant's wildlife hospital in Wales the year before, this was my first seal rescue too.

"Well?"

"The vet's, Harry, in South Street, please. Just round the corner from the house, thank you."

"Rather you than me," he said abruptly. I knew he wouldn't stay mad at me for long. But even though he saw his vocation as healing the sick, to him that meant sick people – animals were a different story. He dropped me off on the busy main street and sat back in the driver's seat, smiling with delight as I struggled to gather up the now wailing seal from the back seat of the car.

"All yours, mate . . . on you go," he said. "Oh, and I take it you won't be out for a drink tonight?" he said smugly. "Sharon will be there, you know . . . Miss Sharon."

"Oh aye . . . that Sharon," I muttered, still struggling with the seal.

"Brilliant." He suddenly cheered up. "Wait till she hears about me and the vicious seal."

"Aye, you're some lad when it comes to seal wrestling, Harry. Listen, thanks mate, won't happen again, eh."

But he didn't answer and was instead staring into space, almost certainly dreaming up his opening lines. I had a strong sympathy for him,

Almost every pre-weaner pup born or abandoned on the busy mainland beaches of Fife would be disturbed or picked up by humans and inevitably end up at Middlebank.

We lost count of the number of Bacardi's wounds that we cleaned and treated with green, antibiotic spray. She was an absolute mess from the injuries inflicted by territorial adult seals and scavenging gulls, and she had to be treated immediately.

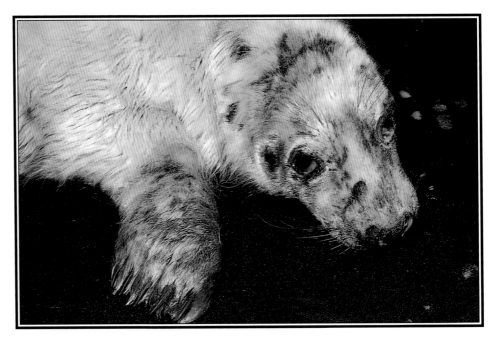

since this time I knew he was doomed to fail. Harry had clearly not noticed that he was by now smelling strongly of that insidious and devastatingly unsexy aftershave that I was later to call "eau de seal".

Harry was absolutely right about me not getting to the pub for a drink that night. Supper was also off the agenda. Over my fifth cup of coffee I stood, as I had done all evening, with Mij in the veterinary surgery, contemplating the new patient now housed rather uncomfortably in a dog kennel.

"What should we call her?" said Mij.

"Bacardi," I replied without hesitation.

She looked puzzled.

"Because a double with coke is just what I feel like right now," I explained.

I put in a call to my old friends Jean and Alan Bryant of the New Quay Bird Hospital in Wales. They were well versed in the rearing of seal pups.

After half an hour of scribbling, and a distinct increase in the anxiety in my voice, I thanked Alan and put the phone down. As I read out the detailed instructions I could see the expression on Mij's face slowly change to panic.

"Liquidised fish in rehydration fluid?"

"Yep," I said.

"Nine times a day?"

"Nine, at least."

"While the seal is trying to bite whatever parts of your anatomy are available?"

"Afraid so. Alan says you have to sit on your knees astride the seal to feed it." We both thought about that for a minute.

"Thick gloves . . . two pairs . . . ?"

"Yep, that's what it says. I've seen it done." I said. "The stomach tube for the liquidised fish is easy. Alan is great at getting the whole fish down later."

"Easy? . . . Easy you say? Tell you what," she said, "I'll do the pouring . . . and, to be fair, I'll stitch back on whatever part of your anatomy the seal tears off you, okay?"

My conversation with Alan had confirmed what I already knew but had never personally experienced – that the business of rearing an aggressive grey seal pup was far from easy. First, a substitute had to be found for the adult female's rich milk. No dairy products came anywhere near the required fat content that was supposed to triple the seal's weight in as many weeks. Our pup weighed only 15 kilograms when she should have been double that.

What we had to do was try to at least maintain her weight and meet her basic nutritional requirements by force feeding. Then, once she had built up some strength, we would introduce her to solid fish – small pieces to begin with and then, eventually, whole. It was only then that she would begin to gain weight.

Perhaps this time I really had taken on too much, but I now felt utterly responsible. It seemed a miracle that Bacardi had survived her terrible ordeal so far and, perhaps in tribute to her strength more than anything, I was determined to give it a try.

We agreed that if Mij and I could get Bacardi through the weekend I would try to arrange for her to go down to Middlebank oiled bird cleaning centre near Dunfermline on Monday. I knew the SSPCA didn't really have a choice; this would be only the first of many more seals dumped on its doorstep, and I knew that, whether it was planned that way or not, the place would soon be functioning as a wildlife rescue centre – with me working there, I hoped.

I searched for some overalls and wellies and found an old pair of leather

Two sets of thick gloves offered some protection but, even so, I felt like counting my fingers after each feeding session. Force feeding was never pleasant for either me or the seal but was essential to the pup's survival.

Opposite: The bristling and fanning of the seal's whiskers was the first indicator of a ferocious snap coming in your direction.

gloves full of holes made by canine teeth. Mij mixed the rehydration fluid and filled a syringe.

I crouched down and studied the seal pup in the kennel. She lay fast asleep, or so I thought until one eye slowly opened to watch me intently. It was so large and dark and clear I could see my reflection in it. She blinked and tears flowed down a wet trail of fur on the side of her face.

We cleaned the pup's wounds and medicated her, under telephone instruction from the vet. Her head and back were covered with so many wounds we had lost count. A steady stream of pus still oozed from her nostrils. "Sorry, lass," I whispered, knowing her force feeding would not be pleasant for anybody, especially her. She tried to open the other eye but it was too swollen. Scavenging gulls had probably tried to peck out her soft eye tissue, and they would have succeeded had she not been discovered that morning by little Toby. She lifted her head and filled the surgery with a ravenous wail.

Tensing my body I made a grab at her hind flippers. As Alan had warned, she whipped round and spat at me in defiance. Blood, pus and urine splattered the surgery. Ignoring her protestations I carefully pulled her backwards to the middle of the floor, where I would be able to get my legs astride her back. Half kneeling, half pouncing, I grabbed her with both hands across the back of her neck and took up my position. She tried desperately to bite me, but my strength on this occasion outweighed hers.

"Okay . . . here goes," I said nervously, releasing my grip on her back with one hand and grabbing her muzzle. This was met with even more ferocious snapping and a call that I felt must have alerted the whole neighbourhood. In fear of my fingers and the stress we were causing her, I grabbed with my other hand until I had control of both jaws. A muffled wail that sounded like someone gargling in a glass of water raised a sympathetic smile on my face.

Mij was now kneeling close by, ready to hand me the fluid-filled syringe with the stomach tube attached. I managed to manipulate my fingers between Bacardi's teeth and get some leverage to open the mouth. Before long I was gazing down a nice pink gullet. I was sweating and puffing.

Mij inserted the stomach tube – until it stopped suddenly only half way down her throat.

"Force it," I said. "Alan says they can close their throats as they do against the water when submerged. We're not there yet . . . keep going."

With a little more pressure Mij got the tube all the way into her stomach and gently delivered the syringe's contents. Bacardi shook her head slightly and gurgled. We sprayed her wounds with an antibiotic spray. Once Mij was out of harm's way I let go of Bacardi's jaws with one hand

and held the back of her neck down again to allow me to let go of the other and remain in control. In a steady motion I stood up and let go completely. Exhausted, she merely croaked and shuffled back into the dog kennel, piddling as she went.

For a short while we watched in silence as she settled back to sleep, clearly happy to feel a full stomach once again. She stretched her flippers and hiccupped as we turned off the light and left her in peace.

Bacardi survived the weekend and so did I, but not without several changes of clothing and plentiful applications of antiseptic and sticking plasters.

I ARRANGED FOR LEAVE FROM MY PART-TIME JOB THAT WEEK SO I COULD MEET MY NEW RESPONSIBILITIES WITH BACARDI, AND SECURED HER RELOCATION TO THE OILED BIRD CENTRE.

Sandra Hogben, the centre manager, was by then a good friend, and was keen to help rear Bacardi. More importantly, she was delighted to offer, on behalf of the SSPCA, unlimited board, lodging and a fine supply of fresh fish. I had been a little coy with the exact details of what was involved and, despite a twinge of guilt, was delighted the deal was now done.

By lunchtime Monday, Bacardi and I were in transit, and the chauffeur was Harry. I was a bit scared to ask, but was pleasantly surprised when he gladly offered his services once again. I suspected that, although not wanting to show it, he had become genuinely concerned about the seal pup.

Nevertheless Harry was very quiet as we set off. I knew all was not well, and I had an inkling as to why.

"So did you have a good night on Friday?" I asked brightly.

"Okay," he mumbled.

"How's Sharon?"

"Well, can't understand it," he said. "Went okay to begin with, we got chatting then suddenly she looked most uncomfortable, kept blowing her nose and started avoiding me like the plague . . . strange girl."

He'd probably have a better chance with Sharon today after a decent shower, but it would have been undiplomatic to tell him.

As we drove inland through the Fife countryside it began to snow, and before long we found ourselves doing 15 kilometres an hour in a howling blizzard. Bacardi was lying on blankets in an old wooden fish box and remained asleep and oblivious. She was clearly still very sick, but the sound of the engine and the rhythm of the windscreen wipers had settled her down.

The darkening weather dulled the conversation until, after a long silence, Harry said, "Why the hell do grey seals give birth in December,

Opposite: Bacardi McNastie, an Atlantic grey seal pup – intelligent, aggressive, inquisitive and appealing – but never cute and cuddly.

anyway? How would a seal pup survive the North Sea in this winter weather?"

"It seems a bit daft, doesn't it? Apparently only about half of the pups born will survive their first winter. But, believe me, they're fighters; they have the personality to defy just about anything mother nature throws at them. They only have one real enemy you know."

"What's that then, whales?"

"Yes, maybe in some countries, but mostly it's us humans." As we drove, I told Harry about grey seals. At the beginning of this century the grey seal population had been plundered for meat, blubber, oil and pelts until there were only about 500 left. With protection their numbers had grown again, but so had the human population and the fishing industry. In the 1970s a seal cull was initiated by the fishing industry, which claimed seals competed for fish stocks, but there was such a public hue and cry that the government stopped it.

"But . . . Vodka . . . Rum . . ." Harry searched for her name.

"Bacardi," I said.

"Aye, double on the rocks . . . whatever. Will she survive?"

"I don't know," I said. "Fingers crossed." We rounded the corner and the oiled bird centre came into view under a blanket of snow. Sandra and three volunteers were awaiting our arrival. For two of them it was the first time they had seen a seal pup. As we carried her across the threshold Barcardi was wailing and piddling, and I noticed once again that expressions were turning from delight to consternation. Two hours later, after a feed that resembled the Great War, we retreated to the office in shock.

Blood dripped off one of my fingers, while the fingers of my other hand held my nostrils shut against the smell of my overalls. For Sandra it was clearly unfortunate she had been to the hairdresser that morning since her bob was now a perm. Together we looked and smelled like we had just been flushed through the local sewage system.

Although the following couple of days were tough, we were fairly content that Bacardi was at least being filled with enough food and we began to feel we were winning the battle. We were more concerned at our inability to remove the very smelly wall covering, nothing short of a new chemical weapon, with which Bacardi was decorating the room that housed her. But after three days our concerns returned firmly to Bacardi, who was clearly and suddenly beginning to go downhill.

We could sense she was unhappy by the absence of wailing resounding around the property and at times over the fields beyond. Her appearance was little to go by because she had, with her many wounds, her discharges and her toilet habits, never looked the picture of health. A hairy trifle

Bacardi was desperately thin, her bones showing under her skin with every heaving, exhausted breath.

pudding with teeth, which had been dropped on the floor, was a fair description. It was very difficult to judge exactly what the problem was. When I went to examine her closely and was met with mere gurgling and almost no resistance we knew it was time to call in the vet.

Aileen Calder, who worked in partnership with her husband Joe Ryan at Dunfermline, was a very competent local vet. She was getting used to the new oiled bird centre's calls for help, but her response this time was one not only of surprise but a little trepidation.

"I'll have a look," she said, "but I have to say I have never been near a seal before let alone treated one. It's a first for me. We don't get many coming in for neutering or to get their nails clipped in our practice. I thought you were only going to deal with oiled birds?"

"Sshh," I said, "we know. Now listen, I know a couple in Wales who have dealt with a number of grey pups. Shall I phone them?"

"That might be helpful. I might speak to them myself later, but phone them now anyway and I'll see you soon, okay?"

I phoned the Bryants once again for their advice.

"Sounds like septicaemia," Alan said. "It's very common, given the extent of the wounds." He asked what antibiotics she was on. "See what your vet thinks, but I recommend a change to something stronger and a higher dose, and check the lungs for pneumonia. But be quick – I've seen those two nasties take a seal pup overnight. Oh, and if you get bitten . . . sorry, I'll rephrase that . . . where you have been bitten, for goodness' sake, clean the wounds carefully – they can pass on some real nasty bacteria. I still have one finger that doesn't work properly."

"Oh, my gawd, Alan," I said, imagining gangrene and amputation.

"All that aside though Darroch, are you having fun? Are you winning?"

"I'll give it my best shot, but the rest is up to Bacardi."

Aileen agreed that it was a combination of septicaemia and pneumonia and that some stronger antibiotics were in order, and injected Bacardi. We left the seal in peace, keeping our fingers crossed.

A week later, after her seventh feed that day, which by now were becoming almost routine and much easier, I sat for a while beside her simply to observe. She appeared to be over the worst now; her wounds were healing and she was clearly responding favourably to the new antibiotics. As she stared up at me with her now huge, dark, fluid eyes I thought of the incredible battle she had fought in her short weeks of life. It was hard to believe an animal that had seemed so close to death on more than one occasion and was up against such odds had so much fight in her.

I wondered why she had got into difficulties in the first place and could not help but think that if her mother had abandoned her prematurely,

Middlebank in the winter of 1990. By then we had a fully functional seal treatment unit.

Overleaf: Stretching and sleeping were a big part of how grey seal pups passed their time, seen here gathering strength for the next round of harassment of the increasingly exhausted staff.

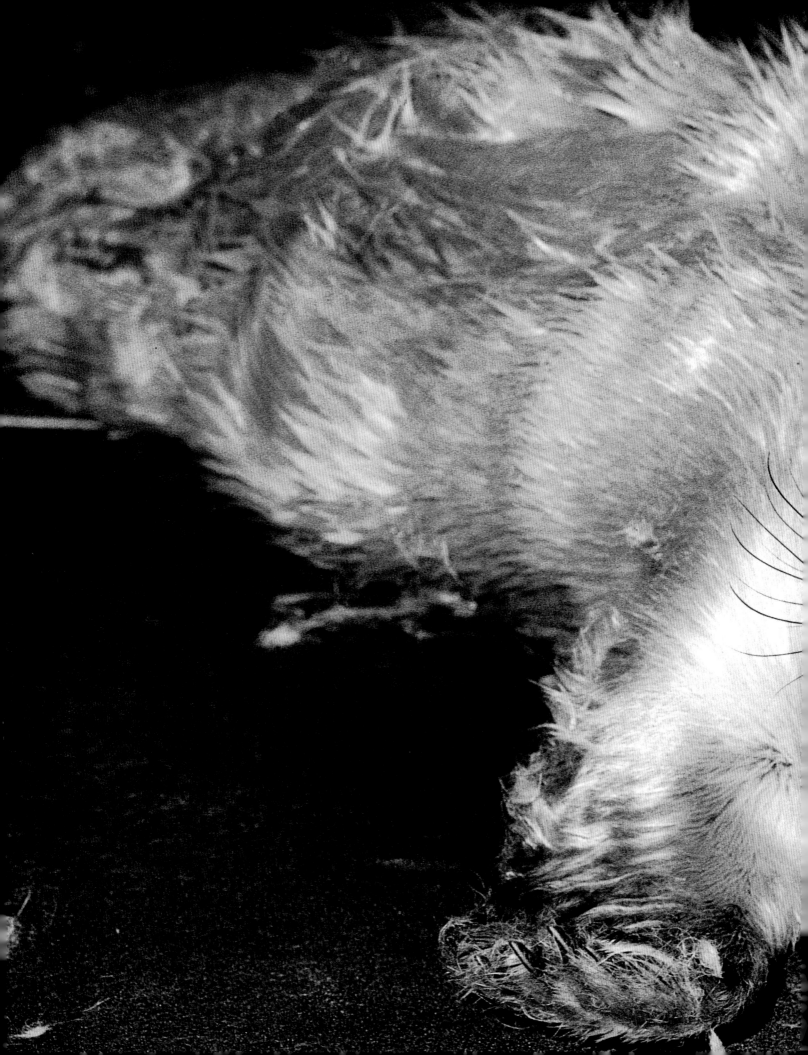

Some essential seal-rearing equipment – waterproofs, gloves, rehydration fluids and syringes, medications, fish, weighing scales and last, but by no means least, a miniature of malt whisky to see you through to the next feed. After so many battles to force feed seals with fish mix, it was three years before I could sit down again to a meal of fish and chips.

Seals create an awful mess. Our clients' quarters had to be cleaned out daily with a steam cleaner. Here volunteer Jim Taylor, wearing eau de seal aftershave, does the honours.

sensing a weakness or deformity in her pup, she had made a poor judgement. But I had to remind myself that quite often a defect or a deformity may not become apparent until weeks after birth. The parent may have recognised this, with some sense that we humans know nothing of or have lost, and acted accordingly.

I had seen this phenomenon many times with ducklings that died suddenly and mysteriously or developed a growth deformity, and I began to feel a little uneasy in the knowledge that there was perhaps a time bomb ticking somewhere in Bacardi that would decide her fate, despite our considerable efforts.

However, the days passed. She was beginning to look healthier and certainly sounded a lot better.

The neighbours more than a kilometre away had only recently been assured that the new oiled bird centre was not in fact some evil place of torture, so human was Bacardi's ravenous wailing. Although she still complained bitterly every time we approached to wrestle her mouth open and insert the stomach tube, we came to the conclusion she did comprehend that the result of the whole bizarre episode was a full stomach and, therefore, it was not all bad. In fact we were beginning to get a little worried that it was all developing into too much of a routine – one that was, for us, very hard work.

Each morning, her room – which always resembled an explosion in a Portaloo – had to be steam cleaned thoroughly, and she herself was hosed down with warm water. This she loved. Except for the occasional eye problem because of dry air, dirt and dust, it is perfectly okay to keep seals out of water. But because water was the medium she was designed to live in most of the time, it was little wonder she took such obvious pleasure in feeling it splash on her body and around her face.

Her first feed was at 8am, with the last of her nine feeds as late as 11pm, and yet all we were achieving was to keep her weight constant. She had to triple it before we could consider release. Our thoughts began to turn very seriously to introducing Bacardi to whole fish in the hope that she would begin eating voluntarily. At nights I was beginning to dream of sitting in the sun in a deck chair by the centre's pool with a double Bacardi on the rocks, throwing its namesake whole herrings and delighting in her ability to catch and swallow them all in one motion. In my dream, as she leaped and wallowed, her great bulk created waves which lapped over my bare feet.

"Oh go on Bacardi, for God's sake." I pulled a dead herring tied to a string past her snout for the umpteenth time that morning. "You're a pain, you hairy little monster. Look, herring . . . food . . . yum, yum, yum."

"Good morning, Donald," said a very clipped posh voice behind me.

The chief executive of the SSPCA, Sir Cameron Rusby, loomed over me. He was looking somewhat perplexed. "I thought they ate a lot of fish?"

"They do, but not dead ones. The problem is this one doesn't recognise it as food. We have to teach her, hence the fish on a string you see."

"Not the fishing industry's best friends, are they?"

"No," I said, dying to say more but stopping myself. We were on slippery ground at Middlebank right now, with a seal in residence. "Should it not be in water?"

"We've been giving her a daily swim in the pools, but she's still too thin to be in water all the time; she would chill. And, besides, she has to be force fed nine times a day so it's as much convenience as anything else."

"Nine," he said. "Who does that then?"

"Me and Sandra and the other volunteers."

"I don't know . . . oiled bird centre one day, seal hospital the next. We should be walking before we run. If you're filling the oiled bird pools with seals, what happens if there's an oil spill?" Luckily Sandra arrived, and they moved off towards the office with an air of considerable strain.

Above and opposite: It was a pleasure to watch Bacardi underwater doing nothing more than simply being a seal.

Overleaf: Bacardi, intelligent grey seal pup that she was, kept herself abreast of local and foreign news and took a particular interest in other rebel causes.

IT WAS A PLEASURE TO WATCH BACARDI UNDERWATER DOING NOTHING BUT SIMPLY BEING A SEAL. WE HAD GROWN SO USED TO HER AWKWARD SHUFFLING AND CLUMSY MOVEMENTS ON DRY LAND THAT NOW WATCHING HER IN WATER WAS QUITE AWESOME. WITH PLAYFUL MASTERY SHE DEMONSTRATED THE ART OF SWIMMING – STREAMLINED, FAST AND AGILE.

Her white pre-weaner coat had now given way to the young adult pelt, and its subtle shades, spots and patterns shone through as the mess and dirt of a landlubber's life dissolved away in the water. She was beginning to look great. Her wounds were healed, she had perfect vision, and my heart was filled with hope. If only she would eat fish on her own. For a while I walked back and forth along the edge of the pool, pulling the fish as I went. I varied the speed, walked, ran, and pounced. "Go on, you stubborn animal." Then, feeling foolish, I realised I was again being watched by the chief executive from a centre window.

Bacardi lay submerged at the bottom of the pool looking at me. The natural fixed seal smile on her face, I thought, began to take on a distinct emphasis.

The days passed and another van load of fish was unloaded. We were beginning to despair. Bacardi still needed to be force fed whole fish five times a day, and by now most of the regular volunteers were helping.

Sandra was not strong enough to handle Bacardi and most days that I was not at my paid job I was at the centre wrestling Bacardi, with Sandra passing me the fish. According to my calculations we had, to date, posted more than 1000 whole herrings down Bacardi's throat. That was an awful lot of fish suppers. She had gained considerable weight but was still only half of the 50 kilograms we had targeted before we could release her.

She was now like a permanent feature in and around the deepest of the oiled bird pools, and although we were not happy about the impasse, Bacardi was. She whiled away the days swimming underwater or simply lazing by the pool. When hauled out she was at times comical to watch. With expressions of sheer delight she would tilt her head to the sun, scratch her tummy or her head with her front flippers, belch, yawn or, at her worst, break wind. She was at times like some delightful couch potato.

I tried to capture her antics with my camera, pausing frequently to attempt the fish on the string routine. But she was more interested in a water fight. It was wonderful to experience this interaction, but, while standing soaked from tip to toe by the walls of water she splashed towards me with her flippers, I could not help but feel worried. We did not want a pet seal and, although she perhaps was not aware of it, there was a far better place and a far better life awaiting her below the ocean waves.

Black Africa ultimatum on 'rebel' tour

by MARTIN BAILEY, AMEEN AKHALWAYA and ALLISTER SPARKS

BLACK African countries are expected to call on England to withdraw from January's Commonwealth Games in New Zealand if their plan to stop the 'rebel' cricketers go to South Africa fails. The issue will dominate a meeting of Commonwealth foreign Ministers opening in the Australian capital, Canberra, today.

Although African sportsmen have previously boycotted sporting fixtures at which teams have played or with sportsmen from South Africa, it is now felt that the withdrawal of New Zealand's invitation would become of their because of a row over the apartheid and ... Commonwealth Games should be avoided.

In South Africa, black opposition to the rebel tour grew...

The Anti-Apartheid Movement said... more than ... group of the ... would ...

HOPE FOR STRICKEN PUPS DETECTED IN THEIR...

MINE SCARE

extract gold on ... using a cyanide ... have raised fears ... environmentalists ... a small spillage ... iously pollute ... best salmon river. ... Scotland, page 4).

AIR PERIL

I blinked as the silvery body of a fish appeared on the surface. To my great surprise and joy there appeared to be a seal attached.

Opposite: Speak no evil perhaps, but she was a devil to feed.

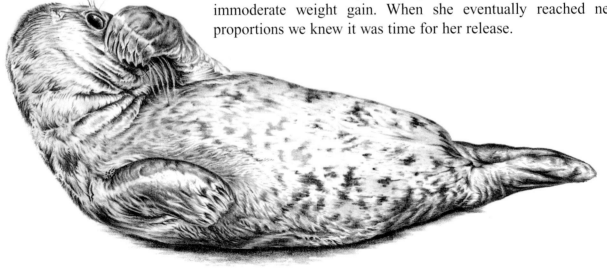

AFTER MORE THAN TWO MONTHS AND 1500 FORCE-FED HERRINGS, I TOOK AN HOUR OFF TO PHOTOGRAPH BACARDI BY THE SIDE OF THE POOL. AS I LAY DOWN AND FILLED MY FRAME WITH HER "IS IT LUNCHTIME?" LOOK, SHE SLIPPED INTO THE POOL. THIS SHE DID EFFORTLESSLY AS IF THE LAND HAD ONLY BEEN BORROWING HER FOR A WHILE.

I lay motionless, anticipating her stealthy attack plan. I knew she would hide on the bottom of the pool for a while, no doubt hoping I would forget she was there. I turned my camera and focused on the surface, awaiting the inevitable explosion of water. Ripples echoed around the pool and faded.

I blinked as a fish tail broke the surface and the silvery body of a whole herring appeared. Moments later, Bacardi's head surfaced, holding the fish tightly in her jaws. I watched in utter disbelief as she flipped her head back, spun the fish round in mid-air and caught it again. It was as if she had mastered the technique long ago. With one bite, half the fish disappeared down her throat. There wasn't even a hint of surprise on her face.

I continued to stare, spellbound. Suddenly she let the rest of the fish fall from her mouth, as if she'd been caught out pretending all this time that she couldn't do it on her own. Bacardi had just pencilled in her release date.

The same evening, a bottle of Bacardi was duly collected and demolished in celebration. It was some bash, and the following morning was spent easing a rather sore head by the pool, throwing in whole herrings and watching with satisfaction as they were hoovered up by an equally ecstatic seal. Over the next three weeks she vacuumed more than 30 whole herrings a day in an expensive but delightful demonstration of immoderate weight gain. When she eventually reached near barrel proportions we knew it was time for her release.

EVERY SEAL THAT I'VE HAD THE PLEASURE OF MEETING HAD ITS OWN PERSONALITY — AGGRESSIVE OR VERY PLACID, QUIET OR VERY VOCAL. SOME, LIKE BACARDI, WERE BONNY; OTHERS WERE DOWNRIGHT UGLY. BUT WHEN IT CAME TO GRASPING THE VERY IMPORTANT AND QUITE SIMPLE FACT THAT FISH WAS FOOD, SHE REMAINED THE MOST INTRACTABLE. I SWEAR SHE WAS THE THICKEST SEAL THAT EVER SWAM THE NORTH SEA. EITHER THAT OR IT WAS SOME ELABORATE JOKE SHE MANAGED TO PLAY ON US. NEVER AGAIN IN MY EXPERIENCE DID A SEAL PUP TAKE MORE THAN 1500 FORCE-FED HERRINGS BEFORE MAKING THE BASIC CONNECTION BETWEEN A FULL BELLY AND A SENSE OF WELL-BEING. ONCE SHE DID REALISE, SHE SEEMED EVEN TO SURPRISE HERSELF WITH THE VARIETY OF PLEASURES A FISH COULD BRING, AND IT WAS BACARDI WHO GOT THE LAST LAUGH.

Like some Hindu princess hidden in purdah, "her Royal fatness" was carried in her sedan chair to the water's edge.

I**T WAS SPRING AND BACARDI HAD BEEN WITH US THREE AND A HALF MONTHS. AS HER RELEASE DATE APPROACHED, WE DECIDED IT WOULD BE A GOOD IDEA TO TAG HER.**

This was fairly straightforward and painless. Instead of the metal ring we used for our avian customers, a plastic ear tag used for cattle, inscribed with her own personal number, was put discreetly through the skin of her webbed, rear flippers. As Aileen attached the tag to a rather disgruntled Bacardi I said a quiet prayer that it would never be recovered again – at least not for a very long time and certainly not without a happy, healthy seal still attached.

We decided that the Eden Estuary near my home town of St Andrews was the best release site. Although the Firth of Forth was only a short drive

Right and opposite: Bacardi peered longingly out towards freedom, every one of her senses anticipating her reunion with the North Sea, wide open and awaiting her exploration.

Bacardi's snout breathed the sea air and broke her last, unseen barrier to freedom. She shuffled forward and looked towards the waves, then from side to side. The moment of return to her natural world had arrived, and we watched with delight as she shuffled down the beach, slid gracefully into the water, slipped further and further into the channel and, finally, was gone.

from the centre and seals were frequently seen there, the water was polluted from ancient sewage outlets, oil refineries and terminals, and we felt we would not be giving her a fair start by putting her there. Although the water was not much better at Eden Estuary she would at least have immediate access to the North Sea, wide open and waiting for her exploration. Research has established that immature grey seals will not usually hang around their own neighbourhood after being kicked out. Like some bitter abandoned human child they will often travel for years before returning home, hardened and aggressive and with a huge chip on their shoulder, to breed. For seals, that is simply survival.

The release was kept low key. Sandra had invited only myself and the other volunteers who had played their parts as surrogate mothers. Triumphantly we carried her across the sand to the water's edge in a huge wooden box with poles at either side, as if she were a Hindu princess. Out in the channel nostrils broke the surface and several pairs of huge dark fluid eyes watched intently as we were quickly outnumbered by inquisitive resident seal spectators. Screeching gulls circled and landed, and there was much human chat and excited laughter. Then we all fell silent, realising the moment had arrived.

The door was swung wide and all eyes were on Bacardi. Her snout was the first thing to appear, tentatively breaking the barrier to freedom. Whiskers twitched and her nostrils sampled the air. She shuffled forwards and looked towards the waves and from side to side. There was a pause, then she exploded out of the box and, with a huge splash, returned to the world where she belonged. I watched in delight as she swam the same distance as the pool and then stopped in obvious surprise. She looked back. A volunteer shouted goodbye, but I knew it was the shore, not us, that Bacardi was looking at. She turned and submerged again, this time resurfacing a greater distance away. She submerged again, and again the distance was greater, until she was lost amongst the seal spectators. Then, almost in unison, their big dark eyes blinked, nostrils closed and they all disappeared into their watery world together.

As I drove back through the Fife landscape, I noticed how green and fresh everything looked and I felt the weight of winter and the strains of the past few months had lifted. I recalled driving with Bacardi to the centre that mid-winter day in the snow. I remembered counting her faltering, hoarse breaths as she lay in the back of the van. And I remembered the 1500 force-fed herrings. I remembered her wailing, her smells and the mess. I remembered her smile and her playful antics. My heart filled with the joy that our encounter with Bacardi had brought us all, and I accelerated, eager to get back to the centre for more.

Typical grey seal habitat, the North Sea. Here, life is fought for and won against great odds – bitter cold, wild storms and sometimes human interference.

UNDER A BLANKET OF THICK FOG TWO NOSTRILS BREAK THE SURFACE OF THE WATER. THEY INHALE AND SAMPLE A CHILL WINTER'S BREEZE. WHISKERS TENSE AND TWO LARGE, FLUID EYES APPEAR. SHE MOVES GENTLY UP AND DOWN IN THE SWELL, LOST. SHE LISTENS . . . AND BEYOND THE MUSIC OF THE RAIN SHE HEARS THE FAINT PULSATING MOAN OF A FOGHORN.

Within a second she breathes out, her nostrils close and she submerges. Her heartbeat automatically slows and her metabolism changes, sparing oxygen until the next resurface. Her streamlined shape shoots through the water, powered by her hind flippers in the direction of the noise. Within a few minutes she surfaces again to breathe and get her bearings.

She swims around the headland towards the breeding colony where she herself was born five years before. This will be her first experience of giving birth. As she creeps into shallower waters, two sentinel gulls stand motionless, watching her quietly from the shore. There is blood on their beaks from scavenging.

She can sense others now. A dark shape larger than her own shadows her movements in the water nearby, and with each resurface the air brings the smell of other seals that have hauled themselves onto land.

Hampered by the fog she tries to negotiate a safe landing. She is a late arrival and most territories are already taken. To find a place of her own she will have to run the gauntlet of other residents, and they will be hostile.

With trepidation, and assisted by a wave, she hauls her bulk onto land. Shuffling awkwardly she eases herself past one female that has also recently arrived. It too is exhausted and still pregnant. It offers little opposition and, since their bodies don't touch, it ignores her. Directly in her path now are three others, each defending its space. They have already given birth and are suckling pups, so if threatened they will be fiercely hostile. Contact is inevitable. The first female whips round towards her, growling in defiance and flapping a flipper in the air. It raises its head high and makes ready to strike. For a while there is a stand-off and they just stare at each other.

She heaves her body forward, and their bodies touch. The reaction this time is ferocious, and teeth sink deep into her blubber. The force of the strike propels her on, and the fight is over. In the only comfortable, unoccupied space she can find she rests and blinks the blood and the sand from her eyes. It's nightfall before she secures a territory. That night her pup is born.

As day breaks, the plaintive, haunting wails of the pups fill the ice cold air. Rain falls heavily through the fog that, for the third day running, shrouds the island. The colony's most recently born pup shuffles uneasily by her side, crying out helplessly. It nudges her huge bulk, feeling desperately with its whiskers for a teat. Nearby, gulls squabble loudly over the discarded placenta and umbilicus.

The pup is at its thinnest now and, despite a thick white fur coat, it will have to find a teat quickly and feed if it is to survive the bitter cold. Guided by instinct it suckles its mother's warm, fat-rich milk, eyes blink slowly in pleasure as its belly fills, its head drops to the sand and the pup joins its mother in dozing. Steam rises from their warm bodies and spouts rhythmically from their nostrils with every deep, contented breath. For two weeks the days seem to merge in rain showers and perpetual, mid-winter darkness. Unaffected by the weather and cold, mother and pup continue their rapid weight transference. With the milk so rich in fat the pup doubles its weight and its mother loses almost a quarter of hers.

In the colony, numbers are decreasing as mothers instinctively abandon their pups after about three weeks and return to the sea, to be again pursued by the dominant bulls and to mate, beginning the process anew.

Meanwhile, the pups, weaned and triple their birth weight, shed their white fluffy coats and, driven by hunger and instinct, head to the sea where they will fend for themselves.

This pup's mother is perhaps young, and this is her first attempt at rearing. Perhaps in hunger, or driven by another urge, she abandons her

It would be nightfall before she secured a territory.

pup too early and runs the gauntlet back to the sea. For days the pup waits, frequently wailing in despair. It grows colder, thinner and more anxious, desperately searching for its mother. It strays into other females' territories and before long becomes the focus for their aggression and hostility. Desperately and awkwardly dragging itself around, it nudges the bodies it encounters, searching for mother and milk. But with each touch comes an explosion of anger. Bitten and shaken, trapped between blubber and rock, it struggles seawards, attacked repeatedly until its white coat runs red.

Tumbling under the surf, instinct and nature take over. Disorientated and in panic it tries calling out but its throat and larynx close tight against water. Panic subsides as it resurfaces, until it feels the stinging of wounds and the bitter cold. Only a third the weight it should be and still in its white pre-weaner coat, it feels the cold intensely and tries to get back on land. Thrashing against the current, it is swept beyond the headland out to sea. Scavenger gulls stand watching, and two follow closely from above.

Now well beyond the island the seal pup drifts with the currents and the swell occasionally pulls it under. Every time it submerges it tries to resurface, sometimes a minute or more later, struggling upwards to the fading light. Well into the darkness it struggles, growing more and more exhausted, until eventually it is washed up close to death onto a beach. Dawn breaks to the excited calls of scavenger gulls.

Hours later, a small boy playing on the beach discovers the pup and the child's mother telephones the St Andrews vet . . .

Two nostrils broke the
surface of the water.

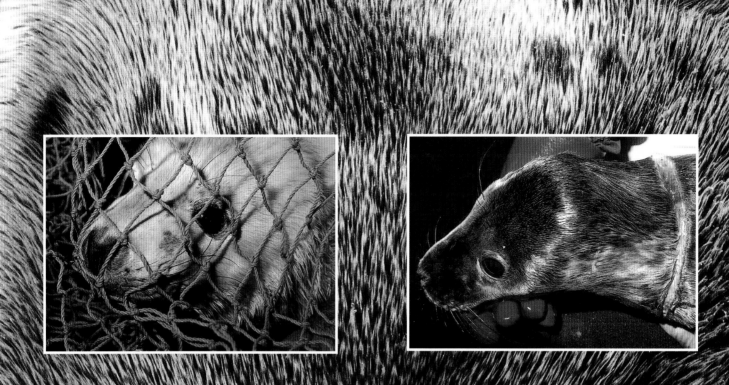

WE DEVELOPED THEMES TO PICK NAMES FOR OUR SEALS — SCOTTISH ISLANDS, DRINKS, CARTOON CHARACTERS AND THE NAMES OF CONFECTIONERY. MY EXPERIENCE OF REARING THESE CREATURES HOLDS SOME PRECIOUS MEMORIES OF NAMES LIKE BACARDI, SKYE, PLUTO AND KIT KAT.

BACARDI'S TAG HAS, AS FAR AS I KNOW, NEVER BEEN RECOVERED. SHE WAS THE FIRST OF THE GREY SEALS AND COMMON SEALS WE HAND-REARED. DURING MY MIDDLEBANK YEARS, FROM 1986 UNTIL 1992, WE RECEIVED 184 SEALS. OF THOSE, 97 WERE RELEASED, 81 DIED AND SIX HAD TO BE HUMANELY DESTROYED.

EIGHT TAGS WERE RECOVERED. THREE UNFORTUNATELY HAD NO SEAL ATTACHED AND WERE WASHED UP VERY SOON AFTER RELEASE, SO WE CAN ONLY SPECULATE ON WHAT HAPPENED. THREE SEALS WERE FOUND DEAD. ONE, SADLY, GOT ENTANGLED IN FISHING NETS AND DROWNED. ANOTHER, A COMMON SEAL CALLED SORREL (HERBS AND SPICES THAT SEASON) WAS OBVIOUSLY A REAL TRAVELLER AT HEART. HER BODY WAS DISCOVERED ON A BEACH IN NORTHERN IRELAND, MORE THAN 1000 KILOMETRES AWAY ONLY 54 DAYS AFTER RELEASE, WHICH MEANS SHE COVERED ALMOST 20 KILOMETRES A DAY. I IMAGINE THE WALLY FORGOT TO STOP FOR LUNCH! THE OTHER, MARTINI (DRINKS AGAIN), WAS FOUND DEAD THREE YEARS LATER — WHICH IS, IN A WAY, ENCOURAGING, THAT SHE LIVED SO LONG.

THE TWO LIVE SIGHTINGS OF MIDDLEBANK SEALS, BOTH GREYS AND RECENTLY RELEASED, WERE ABOUT A YEAR APART. HAWTHORN AND POLO WERE SPOTTED BASKING IN THE SUN AT A COLONY OFF THE NORTH-EAST ENGLISH COAST. GOOD LUCK AND FAIR WINDS TO THEM ALL.

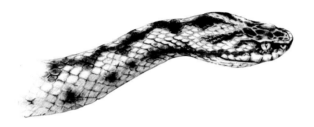

Y-FRONT

A WANDERING ADDER MEETS DESPERATE DAN

IT MAY SURPRISE SOME PEOPLE TO LEARN THERE IS A POISONOUS SNAKE, THE ADDER, FOUND IN THE UNITED KINGDOM, AND THAT IT IS CAPABLE OF DELIVERING A BITE NASTY ENOUGH TO LEAVE THE RECIPIENT FEELING LIKE THEY'VE JUST GONE TWO ROUNDS WITH MIKE TYSON.

Adders generally live in the more remote parts of Scotland on heath and moorland, and are mostly seen only by chance during spells of fine, dry weather when, like lizards, they enjoy basking in the sun. Otherwise they are very hard to find.

Many people believe that snakes lurk in the grass waiting for us, tongue flicking and ready to strike with a poison that will cause instant convulsions and the most hideous death imaginable. Of course it's true that snakes do bite and their venom can kill, but the bottom line is that almost all snakes are equally terrified of human beings and usually they will hear you coming first and slither away. Exceptions arise if they have young to protect or if you are about to step on them, and it is under these circumstances that most bites from adders occur in the United Kingdom.

Although overall quite muted in colour, Y-Front was a beautiful creature up close. The zigzag pattern along his back and subtle herringbone lines were like some intricate tapestry.

The reptilian head, typically flattened and poised.

So, you are generally lucky or, if you like, unlucky to encounter one, and the circumstances through which we received our first wild adder at Middlebank wildlife rescue centre were most surprising and entertaining.

According to the SSPCA inspector who delivered the adder to us, it happened that a certain Mrs Betty McGinty, from a housing estate in Glasgow, was putting out her washing. Maybe she had popped inside to answer the phone or was chatting to a neighbour, but when she got down through the pile of wet laundry, there, under a pair of underpants, she spotted a snake.

Mrs McGinty must have been an exceptional woman. Someone else might have thrown bricks at it or hit it over the head with a spade. Her reaction was not what you might expect. There were, by all accounts, no blood-curdling shrieks, no hysterics and no immediate calls on 999. Not Mrs McGinty – that's Glasgow folk for you.

"Och, the wee thing's lost," she thought, "I'd better call the cruelty man" (as our inspectors are called in that part of the world), and she proceeded to pick it up and put it in a shoe box. Incredibly, it didn't bite her. Perhaps it was too surprised. One of the Glasgow inspectors duly collected it and, unsure what to do, brought it to the centre. He was just a young lad and, like most of the inspectors, was more familiar with stock or domestic animals than wildlife. He delivered the box at arm's length, briefly told us the story, then found an urgent meeting at HQ to attend.

Excited, we opened the box a little warily. I had once come across a nest of baby adders – tiny, beautiful things about 18 centimetres long – but I'd never handled or even seen an adult adder. It was about 75 centimetres long. There it lay, coiled up on the port side of a pair of extra large "Desperate Dan" underpants. As with many wildlife species, it's only by looking closely that one can recognise an adder's real beauty, its subtle colouring and complex design, and appreciate the extraordinary artistry of nature.

Although the design on the underpants was rather impressive, the design on the adder, even from a respectful distance, was more so. It was a beautiful creature, its colouring a wonderful range of browns, with a striking single line of black diamonds the length of its back and a fine herringbone pattern down the sides echoing the Navajo zigzag on top. Adders can range from nearly black to light fawn in colour.

We identified the snake as male and christened him "Y-Front" in honour of his place of discovery, since snakes never look desperate and he was certainly not a "Dan". There was clearly nothing wrong with him – he was alert and anxious to try and get away. We came to the same conclusion as Mrs McGinty: the poor wee thing was simply lost or passing through, and

Opposite: Y-Front at almost life-size.

just happened to make the mistake of using a pile of underpants to hide under. But what he was doing in a Glasgow housing estate remained a mystery.

We decided he should be released as soon as possible, so we set about researching the best place to do so. It's difficult to tell what sort of condition a snake is in unless it is obviously injured, because you can't tell whether it's fat or thin. Y-Front wasn't hurt, and usually snakes (although not so much adders) can last some days without eating. As he was only to be with us a couple of days, we weren't too worried about the adder's refusal to eat.

In the short time available I wanted to photograph Y-Front. He was exquisite, and I knew the contrast of a background of smooth, round grey pebbles would enhance that beauty. I hadn't handled many snakes before, and the idea that this one was poisonous felt weird. But I like snakes and I was fascinated to look at Y-Front close up. At first, I made sure I was wearing big gloves. You hold a snake gently with your thumb on top of its head and finger underneath, so they can't swing around and bite you. You can also grip the tail end, which means, one hopes, that you're in complete control. (Children, please don't try this. In fact, anybody who comes across a boa constrictor anywhere – heaven forbid in your underpants – should not try this at all. I recommend, in that instance, sheer panic, shrill calls for help and the fastest hundred metres you have ever done.)

Once you're holding the head securely, you don't need the gloves. It is preferable to use your bare hands, as this lessens the chance of damaging a snake. In fact you should handle snakes as little as possible, so they are least stressed by the human touch. Y-Front must have been extremely passive for Mrs McGinty to have been able to pick him up. The adder didn't really get annoyed when I was handling him, and never tried to bite me. We tend to think of snakes as slimy, but he felt totally smooth, dry, and soft – almost like skin – and wonderful to touch. His body was very flexible, and if I wasn't also holding his tail he would try to wind himself around my arm as I held him.

While I was photographing Y-Front, he used two methods of dealing with my presence. One defence was to coil and sit immobile, as a way of camouflaging himself, instead of making a run for it. The other was to attempt to slither away, and I would have to retrieve him with the glove. Snakes can move fast, but after years of working in wildlife rescue I was faster.

If you can catch fast-waddling mallard ducklings, as I had learned to do, then you can catch just about anything. You develop reflexes to become as sharp as a cricketer's. On occasion I could reach up and catch an escaping

An adder's skin is like artwork in itself.

pigeon in mid-air, which is not generally recommended because you might damage them. But if it was a case of capturing it or letting it escape I could usually surprise myself. This ability made me realise that at one time all human beings were much closer to creatures, and we can retrain and regain those lost senses.

For Y-Front's release we settled on the Pentland Hills just south of Edinburgh. Adders were known to be found there and it would certainly be far away from any underpants, save those belonging to the occasional courting couple.

Releasing Y-Front was something of an anti-climax. I tipped him out of the box and, without further ado, he simply slithered away into the heather. A moment later it was as if he had never been there. I was left with only some photographs of the adder. Mrs McGinty retains the underpants.

In defence adders will curl up and stay motionless. With Y-Front, this was more for camouflage than as a preparation to strike, but knowing he could deliver a nasty bite, I did not test the theory.

BLUE 51

A GUILLEMOT BEATS THE BLACK DEATH

Guillemot Blue 51, a rugged wee seabird.

WITH THE CHORES FOR THE DAY DONE AND MIDDLEBANK, THE SSPCA OILED BIRD CLEANING CENTRE, FOR ONCE VERY QUIET, I WAS SKETCHING SOME OF THE PATIENTS. BUT MY DRAWING SKILLS WERE RUSTY.

The sleeping eider duck in front of me looked for all the world like a large, brown pudding and my sketches were beginning to look the same. The peace was shattered by the ringing of the telephone. I got a bit of a fright and so did my subject. My pencil point broke on the page and the pudding leapt to her feet huffing and puffing in protest. I had agreed to stand by at the centre and answer the phones, and I rushed off to the office in eager anticipation. What creature might we expect this time?

A voice told me in a very matter of fact way that there had been an oil spill up north and birds were already coming ashore. I felt a shiver down my spine, not initially because of the environmental destruction but from excitement. It felt like I had been preparing for this all my life. To me, being in the front line during an oil spill incident was like being an aspiring

Luckily on this occasion, the vessel was not carrying oil.

Opposite: Two guillemots diving for fish. It is at the point of transition between air and water that contamination during an oil spill takes place.

young All Black who had just been called into a rugby world cup final. It was my chance to put into practice what I had been dreaming about since I was a boy, but on a mammoth scale.

"How many birds?" I asked, with barely controlled excitement. My mind was racing ahead already.

"A lot," said the voice. "I have a van full already and the calls keep flooding in. Can you take them?"

"Yes, of course, brilliant. I mean . . . I think so . . . but I'm only a volunteer here, I'll have to let everyone know . . . give me all the details." I scribbled away.

The spill was patchy, but was affecting a large area of Dornoch Firth 250 kilometres away in north-east Scotland. It was suspected to be crude oil from a tanker illegally flushing out its tanks at sea. Weather conditions were poor, there was an onshore wind, and they were expecting large numbers of seabirds to be affected. A major oil spill response had already been put into effect, and as part of that we were immediately put on standby. We were to make ready and await further news.

With my heart racing I put down the phone, and immediately picked it up again. "It's showtime," I whispered to myself. "Now, find Sandra."

Within the hour Sandra, myself and a few volunteers were trying to remain calm and ready ourselves for the worst. There was an intense atmosphere of excitement and purpose, and it was clear I was not alone in my feelings. This was our first major oil spill incident and was, after all, the centre's *raison d'être*. Would we cope? Would the centre prove its worth?

THE MOST COMMON VICTIMS OF OIL SPILLS AT SEA AROUND THE COAST OF SCOTLAND ARE THE AUKS, A FAMILY OF RUGGED LITTLE SEABIRDS THAT INCLUDE THE GUILLEMOT AND THE RAZORBILL. THEY ARE ABOUT THE SIZE OF A PENGUIN AND ARE, INDEED, THE NORTHERN HEMISPHERE'S EQUIVALENT. BUT, UNLIKE PENGUINS, ALL AUKS CAN FLY. AND THEY ARE AS GOOD UNDER WATER IN THE PURSUIT OF FOOD, AS THEY ARE IN THE AIR, IN THE PURSUIT OF TRAVEL. WHEN OIL CONTAMINATES THE WATER'S SURFACE, IT IS THE FREQUENT TRANSITION BETWEEN AIR AND WATER THAT LANDS THE AUKS IN TERRIBLE TROUBLE.

IN THE DAYS OF MY INVOLVEMENT WITH OILED WILDLIFE I TRIED TO KEEP A COUNT OF THE NUMBER OF BIRDS I HANDLED. BUT NOW, AFTER 20 YEARS IN THE BUSINESS OF THE BLACK DEATH, WHAT I REMEMBER ARE NOT NUMBERS AND SPECIES BUT SAD AND DEATHLY IMAGES — BLACKENED BODIES STREWN ALONG THE TIDE-LINES ON EVEN THE REMOTEST BEACHES, DISTRESSED BIRDS IN BOXES AND CAGES, AND DEAD BODIES PILED ALONGSIDE THE REFUSE. AT TIMES IT HAS LOOKED LIKE AVIAN GENOCIDE.

For every out-going call Sandra Hogben, the centre manager, made to organise volunteers and supplies there were five in-coming, from SSPCA headquarters, the public and the press. This was building to be a major disaster, and we were seen as one of the frontline response headquarters for oiled wildlife. The non-oiled wildlife already in care were fostered out to clear as much space as possible. The scene unfolding was like the midnight evacuation of a hospital after a fire alarm.

As I crouched in the foyer sorting boxes to be sent up to Dornoch, I glanced up at the contents of a passing cage and was confronted by a rather disgruntled hedgehog. Like a confused old-age pensioner woken from his peaceful slumber and unable to see much through his bleary nocturnal eyes, he pointed his nose to the heavens and sniffed the air to find out what all the commotion was about. "Sorry, mate," I said ruefully as he disappeared out the door.

Gradually, as midnight approached, the telephone calls became less frequent and since the first batch of birds would not arrive from Dornoch until the following morning there was little else we could do except wait and try to get some sleep. On a makeshift bed in Sandra's house I tried to sleep, but I could only listen to my breathing and stare into the darkness, my mind racing. Kickoff was approaching.

By morning, all hell broke loose. Van loads of pitiful oiled creatures, sick, dead and dying, had to be unloaded and booked in to the centre.

"Two guillemot, both alive," I said, grabbing one of the terrified birds. Shirley scribbled in the log book and handed me a blue plastic ring.

"Blue, number 51," I said, placing the ring round its leg. I felt its breast bone and placed it on the scales. "Two hundred and seventy-five grams," I said, and Shirley scribbled. I placed the bird between my knees and reached for one of the syringes another volunteer was filling. Prising open the guillemot's beak I carefully inserted a catheter down its throat and into its stomach, attached the syringe and gently squeezed, watching the warm hydrating fluid slowly disappear.

The bird shook its head and swallowed repeatedly as I let it go, appearing to relish the fluid which eased its burning throat and filled its empty belly. A short time later it would be given more medication to further ease the burning and limit the damaging effects of ingested oil. Once the birds were indoors the oil on their feathers would dry quickly. That meant a decrease in the amount of poison they would ingest through preening.

Blue 51 was placed in a cage inside one of two reception rooms to build up enough strength to be washed. It is unwise and potentially fatal, with the birds in such a weakened state, to start cleaning straight away,

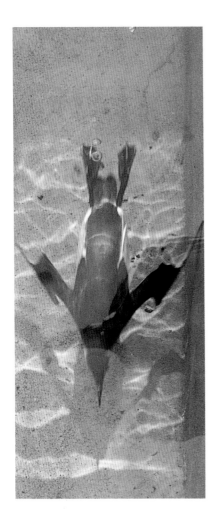

The guillemot's constant diving in search of fish means repeated exposure to surface oil slicks.

Opposite: Once coated in oil the birds lose their water-proofing and, unable to stay afloat, will try to reach land. These are the lucky ones — most never make it and drown at sea.

By morning van loads of pitiful oiled birds were beginning to arrive. These animal ambulances carried a constant cargo of suffering.

especially if the oil is heavy, like crude oil. But if the contaminant is lighter and more toxic – like petrol, which is absorbed quickly through the skin – it must be removed immediately. Some species or individuals adapt very poorly to any form of captivity and their only hope is an immediate clean.

Cages and rooms were filling fast, and by the end of the day Blue 51 had been joined by more than 100 other birds. Most, as expected, were auks – guillemots and razorbills – but they were joined by small groups of seaducks and other seabirds called divers. By the time they arrived, many victims were so soiled they were almost unrecognisable. Thick, black crude coated the boxes, the birds, and our gloved hands. It seemed to get everywhere, even into our lungs, as the pungent, deathly smell permeated the centre.

For all of us, even those who had been treating sick and injured wildlife for years, it was distressing but still exciting and utterly absorbing. I had never felt such a concentrated sense of purpose in my life and, despite the chaos and the suffering, I felt totally at home. The outside world had disappeared and only one thing mattered – the birds.

It very soon became clear, though, that the world had not disappeared. In fact half of it had suddenly turned up on the door step. When I walked outside I was confronted by a lengthening queue of reporters, TV crews and members of the public.

While Sandra alternated between feeding birds and feeding the cameras I helped answer the telephone, which shrilled more constantly than any bird. We soon realised that we would really struggle to cope with a disaster of such magnitude without help, and, accepting the fact that we were all too new to this game, we decided to call in the cavalry.

Later that night two RSPCA wildlife officers, Tim Thomas and Colin Booty, arrived. They both had years of professional experience with oiled wildlife and could undoubtedly show us the light at the end of a rapidly lengthening tunnel. I was keen to meet these two men who had somehow managed to accomplish what I aspired to myself: employment in wildlife rehabilitation. Our meeting in their hotel that night proved a little strained. Perhaps the seasoned professionals had forgotten we all have to start somewhere and, confronted by a new centre manager and three green volunteers, of which I was the one with the unpronounceable name, they retired early.

Staring in silence at our pints in the hotel bar, Sandra, Shirley Jenkins, Callum McGregor and I felt more than a little deflated, but no less determined to prove them wrong. Shirley and Callum were regular volunteers at the centre, and together the four of us formed a nucleus at Middlebank throughout this episode.

We returned briefly to the centre to check on the birds before retiring to bed ourselves. I was the last to leave and before doing so I checked the birds once more.

As I stood under the gaze of a hundred oiled birds there was a strange and penetrating silence. Many sat with their head feathers puffed up, heads drooping, eyes dulled – the body language of avian depression. To me, there was no doubt of their suffering, no doubt of their emotions, no doubt of their feelings. And in that silence under their gaze I had never felt so humble or so ashamed, not of who I was, but of what I was. It had been a long, demanding, emotional day and was to be the first of many.

I raced to the centre next morning in eager anticipation. With so many more volunteers arriving I was keen to make my mark. I knew I had a lot to offer, and I also wanted to be first in the queue for our seconded experts' tuition. I was immediately confronted by a small pile of dead bodies outside the reception room. I looked at the leg bands and thankfully recognised none.

"Any more?" I asked Shirley.

"Two others in reception two, but that's it. Could be worse."

Tim and Colin were in the office with Sandra having a meeting.

"Hello again," said Tim looking a little uneasy. "Ah . . . er . . . Derrick, isn't it?"

"No, Darroch – roch as in loch and not door lock," I said, almost automatically.

"Okay, okay," said Tim, laughing, "I know we're English but we're not planning an invasion."

I was glad we had broken the ice. For the best part of that morning Shirley and I supervised the arrival of more birds while Sandra showed the experts around and talked tactics. By lunchtime they too were in overalls. Another batch of birds arrived, shadowed this time by a TV crew and another newspaper reporter.

I went into one of the reception rooms to help Callum medicate survivors. I spotted Blue 51 looking right at me. "See that one?" I said to Callum, pointing at Blue. "That one will live, look at the eyes." Callum merely raised his eyebrows and continued his work.

Tim stuck his head around the door. "What are you up to just now? Have you got a minute?" he asked me.

We went into one of the post-wash rooms at the far end of the building which, although designed to house birds before being put outside on the pools, was now set up for a group of divers – seabirds about the size of small geese – which were too big for cages. The room had been darkened and there was silence except for the hum of the air heater.

Unloading the box. For any injured creature, that first human contact must be terrifying.

Blue 51 was our 51st
guillemot patient in a total
of over 200 birds received
during this one spill. But I
wonder how many more have
been victim to the Black
Death.

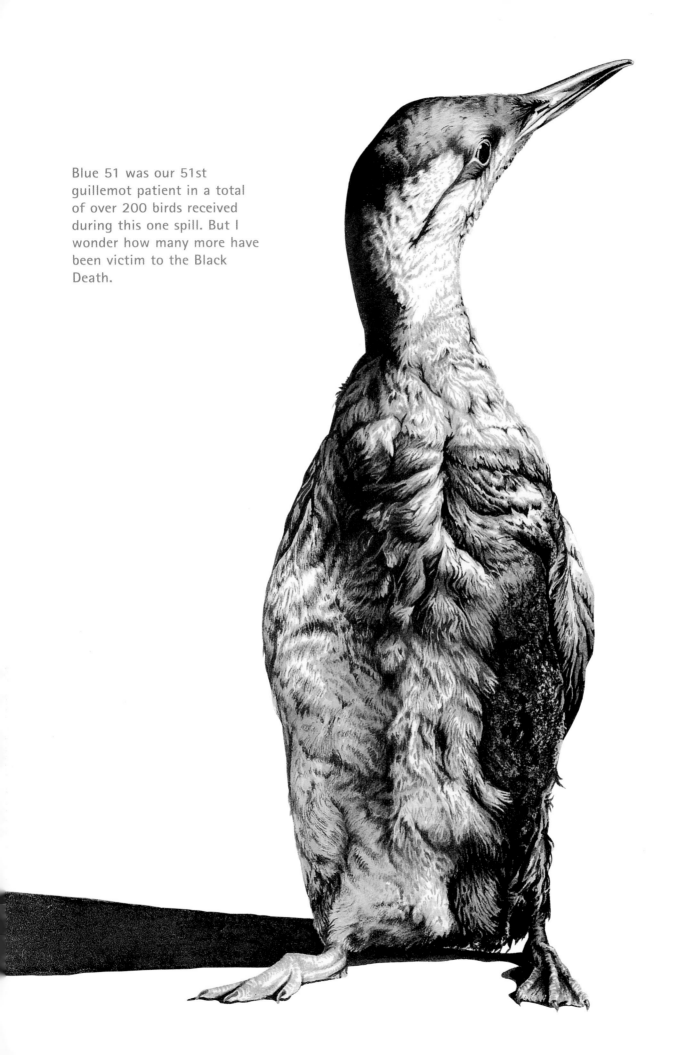

"Divers," said Tim, "are beauties, but a nightmare to rehabilitate. You see this bowl of food you put in?" he whispered.

I nodded.

"Wrong," he said.

"Why's that?"

"They're not like guillies; they're a bit thick and don't recognise a dead fish when they see one, real gourmet eaters. But there is a solution."

"What's that?"

"Get a tray, not a bowl, fill it with shallow water and let just a few dead fish, really fresh, float about. The movement often stimulates them." I was off immediately to sort it out.

With no let up in the number of birds still being brought to the centre, the possibility we would exceed the number of birds Middlebank was designed to manage was causing concern. "We're almost full now, 275 last count," said Sandra with a distinct air of anxiety.

"So what if we get double that, we could surely find the space?" I said.

"My thought exactly," she said, "but unfortunately not one that's shared."

"Why, what are Tim and Colin saying?"

"They are quite adamant that should we go over we should start getting more selective."

"What, and start destroying the weaker ones?"

"Yes, but they are the experts, and there is no getting away from the fact we are new to this situation and they're probably right." For the remainder of the day I pondered on the predicament. It was obvious Tim and Colin were right, but I came to the conclusion their suggestion was also to prove a point.

They obviously felt that the general approach was overly sentimental, and wanted to point out that for an oiled wildlife response on this scale to be successful it had to be steered by hardened professionalism and not sentimentality. Only through the right approach from the beginning would our abilities improve and limitations decrease in the future.

I had to go back to St Andrews for work the following day. Everyone knew where I had been and I could hardly throw a sickie from my part-time job with the council after I'd been plastered over the front page of the newspaper. "I'll call you tomorrow," I shouted as Sandra dropped me at the station. I dragged myself aboard the train. The carriage was warm and empty. The seats for once looked huge and inviting. Within a second I had nestled in, sat back and closed my eyes. As we got under way again the carriage rocked like a cradle and lulled by the quiet rhythmic clatter of its wheels I began to drift asleep.

After some initial first aid, we put the birds in cages in a pre-wash room to build up their strength before we started the stressful business of cleaning.

We had to find boxloads of fish to feed so many birds.

Almost subconsciously I was aware of the train grinding to a halt to pick up more passengers, and was suddenly shocked awake by a young female voice at high volume.

"Ooohhh, what's that smell?" said the voice.

"Oh, shit," I thought. I realised that of course it was me.

I had been liberally covered in fish and bird poop all day and no longer noticed that I was smelling something like Billingsgate fish market on a very hot summer morning. I listened as the girls found a seat, but I couldn't bear to look at them, and pretended to be asleep as they discussed me in loud voices.

"Errrr . . . smells like fish."

"Stinks, eh?"

"Do you think someone's farted?" and there was a barrage of giggling.

I screwed up my face, hoping they would either go away or that my seat would swallow me up. Sadly, neither occurred.

"Do you think it's that man?" came the inevitable, with an explosion of high pitched laughter.

"Oh, my God," I thought, "please beam me up Scottie."

The laws of probability took over and decreed that two schoolgirls would not sit in one place for long. As the train approached the next station they left, and I heaved a sigh of relief. For the rest of the journey I sat in uneasy anticipation of every station bringing more travellers. Fortunately I was spared further embarrassment.

The birds were not the only creatures that were exhausted. Like them we could hardly keep our eyes open.

FOR THE NEXT TWO DAYS I RELUCTANTLY WENT TO WORK AS A DESIGNER AT THE LOCAL COUNTRY PARK, BUT ALTHOUGH MY BODY WAS THERE MY MIND WAS NOT. AS SOON AS I COULD I PHONED THE CENTRE TO CONFIRM MY RETURN THE FOLLOWING DAY. SHIRLEY ANSWERED, AND I COULD TELL SOMETHING WAS WRONG.

"We reached capacity this morning, and . . ." She trailed off.

"Don't tell me, the needles are out in force and birds are being destroyed?"

"Afraid so."

"Uh huh . . . . How's Sandra?"

"Pretty upset."

"Listen, there's one in pre-wash, guillemot, Blue 51, can you make sure . . . ?" But I stopped myself mid-sentence realising I was behaving exactly as the experts warned us not to. "Ah, never mind. Listen, I'll be back there about mid-morning tomorrow, okay?" I said and put the phone down.

Without realising it, or perhaps because it felt so right, I was becoming totally absorbed by the spill and the centre. There was nowhere else I wanted to be, nothing I'd rather be doing. Even though I was just a volunteer, I felt I belonged there. After a fairly sleepless night I couldn't wait to board the train the next morning and get back into the thick of it.

At Middlebank, I took an unadvertised check on Blue 51. He or she was not only still alive but was full of life, sitting up and dipping its head towards an empty food dish. A bird let out a shrill call, simply announcing its being. Although it was clear some birds had not survived, I felt encouraged.

The centre seemed a little more orderly, as new volunteers moved from room to room with newspapers, tubs of fish, mops and buckets. Fewer birds were now arriving – most had turned up within the first four days of the spill. Birds that had not reached the shore and been picked up by then were almost certainly dead.

That day, with Tim and Colin's guidance, our attentions turned to the actual cleaning of the birds.

There was little mention of the selective killing of the weakest birds by lethal injection the day before, and although there was a slight hint of resentment in the atmosphere it was generally accepted that the action was correct. With the intake figures now hovering around our maximum capacity, we had given ourselves the best chance of pulling the whole effort off.

But it was still early days, day six of the crisis. We'd had to wait for the birds to build up strength before attempting to wash them, and as yet not one bird had been cleaned.

"Where's Darruck?" said Tim as he came through the office door.

"Having a coffee and thinking of changing his name," I said.

"Ahh, you layabout, welcome back. Fancy cleaning a bird?"

"Bloody right," I said dumping my coffee on the table and reaching for my wellies.

"I'll go and find Shirley and tell her she's with Colin on the other sink."

We entered the reception room and Tim again ran through the procedure for selecting a bird for cleaning. "Look for the way they're standing and at their eyes first. Pick one, take it out, then check the breast bone for condition and the wing beat for strength. We only want the strongest, okay? Go for it."

Without hesitation I opened a cage and took out Blue 51. "I reckon this one is strong enough, had my eye on it for a while."

It was clear by his pecking that he had plenty of fight and was an ideal candidate. As we left pre-wash and went down to the wash room, decked

We could tell from how a bird was standing, its wing-beat, the shape of eyes and weight whether it was strong enough to undergo cleaning.

Hot, soapy water seemed to relax rather than frighten the birds as they felt encrusted grime float from their matted feathers.

out in cumbersome waterproofs that squeaked and groaned as we walked, we must have looked more like a crisis team at NASA than staff at a wildlife hospital.

We entered the wash room, showerheads burst into life, the sink billowed with steam and my first professional lesson on bird cleaning began. Tim instructed me to place the bird in a basin of hot, soapy water in the sink.

"Bloody 'ell that's hot," I remarked.

"It has to be," said Tim. "They have a higher blood temperature than us and the water should be hand hot."

Blue struggled a bit but seemed to relax when he felt the warm water flood around his body, even attempting to shake his folded wings to bathe. For a creature that hates even the slightest grime on its feathers, it must have seemed like heaven to be bathing after being covered in oil and excrement for over a week.

"Your job as handler," said Tim, "is to hold the bird properly and securely for the cleaner and monitor its condition. You must make sure that if soap gets in its eyes, if it swallows soapy water, or if it seems seconds away from a coronary, you at least let me know so that something can be done about it. My job as cleaner is the systematic and total removal of the oil, every last drop of it." This is perhaps a simple concept in theory, but it is often extremely complex in nature. Co-op green washing up liquid is the nationally accepted decontaminant, and the local supermarket cheapie is just about as good on oiled birds as it is on dishes. But because it is so chemically simple and uncomplicated – removing grease and leaving nothing, including itself, behind – it does not always work.

Some oils, and you don't know until you clean the first bird, can prove very stubborn and sometimes darn right impossible to get off. As we cleaned, Tim told me of one occasion when they had 200 birds covered in a fraction of oil that would simply not come off. After considering every option they had no alternative but to destroy all the birds. "Doesn't happen often," said Tim, "but it can happen."

As Blue 51's feathers were gently agitated, the water quickly turned chocolate brown and the soap suds fizzled away. It was clear this type of crude was reacting just as we wanted it to. I was amazed at how much oil was coming out. We poured the third basin of what looked like chocolate mousse down the sink into a special disposal system and reloaded with more soapy hot water, and were still not even a quarter of the way through the job.

White feathers started re-emerging through the filth, like sunshine emerging from behind cloud. I was filled with hope. Perhaps this bird Blue, and the others, would survive despite this ordeal and our efforts would prove successful.

After 45 minutes of cleaning Tim was confident all the oil was gone, but the process was far from complete. Had Blue been simply manually dried and put out on the pools, or, even worse, released it would have been fatal. Detergent, although effective in removing contaminant oil, has exactly the same effect on the feathers' own waterproofing. The second part of the cleaning procedure is called proofing. Hot water, at high pressure, is jetted through a shower head onto the plumage. Every feather is thoroughly rinsed and the more water you spray on feathers the drier the bird becomes. Feathers, if clean and well-maintained, are perfectly waterproof. Look at a feather under a microscope and you will see millions of tiny barbs and barbules which zip neatly together in one of nature's greatest designs, one that provides not only waterproofing but warmth and flight.

As I continued to carefully manipulate Blue's body into position for Tim

Once all the oil was removed the birds were rinsed thoroughly. This is called proofing.

A squeaky clean great northern diver. Proofing was like magic; suddenly droplets of water stood out like diamonds on the once again watertight feathers.

to proof, the feathers almost magically began to repel the water, becoming literally squeaky clean. He then directed a fine mist instead of a jet of water. Like tiny pearls and diamonds the water sat on the surface of the feathers. It looked magical. At this stage, we tested constantly for water-tightness. When Tim, to demonstrate, merely touched a feather with one soapy finger the pearls of water collapsed and soaked into the feather, indicating the presence of detergent. Blue paddled his feet and agitated his wings furiously, panting a little with fatigue.

Once placed on clean paper and away at last from my grip, Blue shook his entire body and began to preen furiously. To birds, preening is one of life's essential activities, and, despite my presence, Blue did so with almost total concentration.

The whole cleaning process had taken a total of one and a half hours to complete. One hundred percent clean again, Blue was by now very tired, but obviously felt relief and considerable comfort with his feathers returned to their proper state. Celebrating with one of those shrill exuberant guillemot calls, his spirit for life had clearly returned. Blue was placed in a warm and pristine post-wash room to rest overnight before going outside to the pools.

By the end of that day we had cleaned six birds. Two of those I had done myself, with Shirley doing the handling. Despite the physical discomfort, I had enjoyed every minute. Each bird cleaning became like an exam or a piece of artwork, receiving my total concentration and attention to detail.

By Day 10 of the crisis we had received 359 birds in total, 238 were still alive and 19 had been cleaned. Outside several bags of dead birds awaiting proper disposal lay testament to those that had died.

Despite the fact we were all still new to this business, I felt we had formed a solid and competent team, and as Tim and Colin left I also felt confident we had dispelled any doubts they had so clearly demonstrated on arrival. We were enormously grateful for their guidance and instruction, but we realised that now it really was up to us and there was still a very long way to go.

Although the guillemots and razorbills were proving resilient and the oil was coming off them completely, we were quickly learning that some of the species in our care were not doing so well. The divers were proving a major problem since they were still not feeding very well and their feet, which were so seldom out of water, were rapidly drying up and blistering. Although treatment with a moisturiser was possible before cleaning, once cleaned, nothing, not even the grease from your sandwiches, was allowed to recontaminate the birds' feathers.

We decided that they should be washed immediately to get them back into water, even though they were still weak and not really prepared.

For five hours we struggled to clean one great northern diver, yet, even after meticulous and prolonged agitation of the feathers, areas simply would not clean. Watching the bird practically expiring in my hands, I quickly proofed it, oil patches and all, and placed it in the post-wash room to rest.

I became moody and depressed and was quickly learning that I was not necessarily always going to meet my own exacting standards. We telephoned Tim, who was not surprised to hear from us and was already sending us a cleaning agent called BMD (biodegradable marine detergent) for those extra stubborn patches. It was strong stuff to be used very carefully and in small quantities, since there were doubts that it would rinse off completely.

When it arrived the following morning we went into battle once more. The first diver had died overnight, and I couldn't help but feel responsible. I reminded myself I was not the maniac responsible for spilling the oil in the first place and felt a little better. But when the second diver died suddenly after two hours of washing and only minutes from completion I cursed loudly as I carried its limp body out of the wash room. I went to the pools, wanting to be alone, and sat for a while, the diver's body on my lap, watching Blue 51 swimming about with ease.

Blue waited for his food dish to fill again like magic.

"This oil business, Blue . . . it ain't easy, is it?" I said to the attentive little bird. Blue merely jumped out of the pool and shuffled towards his empty food dish, bowing his head towards it and waiting for it to fill again like magic. He had been out on the pool now for two days and was doing very well.

We were all beginning to feel stressed and exhausted and had all ignored a warning from the experts not to overstretch ourselves. With many problems to face and the press anxious for the images and figures of success, we were becoming a little exasperated. So, to ease the strain and keep the cameras happy, we decided to take a brief rest from the intensity of the cleaning and turn our attentions to the release of the first batch of survivors.

KNOWING THAT THE FIRST RELEASE WOULD INEVITABLY HAVE TO BE A FORMAL, SOMEWHAT STAGED AFFAIR, WE SPLIT THE AWAITING BIRDS INTO TWO GROUPS – THE FIRST FOR OFFICIALDOM AND THE CAMERAS, THE SECOND IN SECRET FOR OURSELVES.

On Day 13 there was an extra special atmosphere. The birds on the pools became agitated with all the activity and were swimming warily around together, occasionally skittering off in panic and sending showers

THE SECOND PART OF THE CLEANING PROCEDURE IS CALLED PROOFING. HOT WATER, AT HIGH PRESSURE, IS JETTED THROUGH A SHOWER HEAD ONTO THE PLUMAGE. EVERY FEATHER IS THOROUGHLY RINSED AND THE MORE WATER YOU SPRAY ON FEATHERS THE DRIER THE BIRD BECOMES. FEATHERS, IF CLEAN AND WELL-MAINTAINED, ARE PERFECTLY WATERPROOF. LOOK AT A FEATHER UNDER A MICROSCOPE AND YOU WILL SEE MILLIONS OF TINY BARBS AND BARBULES WHICH ZIP NEATLY TOGETHER IN ONE OF NATURE'S GREATEST DESIGNS. ONE THAT PROVIDES NOT ONLY WATERPROOFING BUT WARMTH AND FLIGHT.

Before release each bird was fitted with a leg ring. By ringing birds we could build up a picture of our success rate, but we hoped, of course, that a banded bird would not come into human hands again.

Opposite: I could have given up what seemed a hopeless task, but seeing Blue still alive and swimming happily was some consolation in this awful mess.

of water into the air. This created an avian buzz that extended back indoors to the pre-wash rooms, from which some of the many remaining birds attempted to reply.

Armed with a net and a watch, Callum and I sat by the pool. Our job was to test the birds' waterproofing and assess their suitability for release. On release, given the time of year, most of these guillemots and razorbills would not touch dry land again for two or three months, before returning to the cliffs to breed.

We kept the 12 guillemots and a razorbill on the water for almost an hour, ready to rescue any that were clearly sinking. Only two birds had to be removed from the water. For them, a few more days would hopefully see the small but significant wet patches on their plumage restored, with further preening, to their proper state. They had been observed to sink only slightly, but given several hours on the icy cold, turbulent North Sea they would almost certainly drown.

"What are you doing?" said Callum. "That one looks perfect."

"That one," I replied, "is Blue 51. Selfish, I know, Callum, but I want to hold him back. I want to see his leaving in person, not on the news. If I'm not going on this release, neither is he. I'll let him go with the other lot myself."

Each bird was passed to the ringer, Ian Poxton, who weighed it in a bag then expertly placed a numbered metal ring on one leg. On each was a personal ID number and an address to which to send its number when and if the birds were captured again or their bodies discovered. This way we had the best chance of finding out what happened to our birds after release and we hoped, over time, to build up a picture of our long-term success.

Before long our first batch of survivors was boxed and ready to go. I was a little regretful at staying behind, but knowing we'd have our own unofficial release ceremony the following day, I was glad to accept Sandra's request that I keep an eye on the place while she went and exercised her official duties.

Aside from Callum, I was not particularly well acquainted with the remaining volunteers. Having been officially open for only four months, Middlebank had not yet established a large pool of regulars. In our naivety we had rarely questioned whether anybody, especially those that could come during the day, were up to the job.

One of the volunteers on this day was a young man I will never forget. Tam (not his real name) had joined us early in proceedings and was gladly taken on. I was practically flattened one morning when I was walking into the centre as he was walking out and we collided. I am not exactly small

Previous page: After cleaning and a rest the birds were placed outside on clean, specially built pools.

To test their waterproofing each bird was kept on the water's surface for about 40 minutes. The candidate on the left had passed and was clearly waterproof. The bird in the middle is starting to sink and needs further attention; for this bird, release at this stage would be fatal.

myself, but Tam, although the same age and height, was twice my width. Once I reinflated myself, I felt annoyed that during and after my flattening he'd just laughed. I brooded over the incident, watching him handle birds with all the finesse of a cement mixer, and couldn't control my dislike and distrust. Knowing it was really none of my business, I couldn't stop myself expressing my doubts to Sandra.

She pointed out that he was a volunteer – just like me – and perhaps all he needed was the chance to learn and change. By the end of the week we found out Tam had been in trouble with the law. His probation officer visited, persuaded Sandra that he was reliable and could be trusted, and encouraged her to give him regular work as a volunteer.

So on the day of the first oiled bird release I felt honoured having the responsibility to guard the place, but, with Callum on his way home with a migraine and the others away to lunch, I was not so delighted to be left alone in the company of Tam.

At times, I also had an inexplicable feeling of being physically threatened by him. Two days earlier my mother's dog, who is one of the friendliest mutts in the world, refused to go near him, barking at him and placing her tail firmly between her legs. She was clearly aware of something we less astute humans were not.

Perhaps sensing my disdain, he avoided me and left me to eat my lunch alone in the office. The telephone and the door bell were for once, with all the attention focused on the first official release, relatively quiet. Tam passed the office window twice, very quickly, while I ate my sandwiches. The silence was strangely ominous and I decided I had better check on big Tam.

Indoors and the wash rooms were in order, and I walked out into the sunshine and gripped the wire mesh to look over the pools. My body flooded with shock. Where I was expecting to see the remaining birds swimming or sitting in the sun I was confronted with what looked like dead bodies scattered around the edges of the water and in the pool, and only two stood huddling nervously in the corner. For a moment I couldn't believe my eyes. I fumbled with the door handle and stumbled towards the birds.

Two were floating face down in the water and another lay gasping on the side. Grabbing the bird and looking at it more closely it looked for all the world as if someone had pumped air into its head. Its eyes were almost bulging from its sockets and blood was oozing from its mouth. My heart sank when I saw a blue ring. I scraped at some faeces and the figure 72 appeared. The bird gave a gasp and its body went limp. My mind was in turmoil and racing as I moved about, reaching for the dead bodies in the pool, searching for ring numbers. Still having not found what I was looking for, I turned to the pair huddled in the corner, picked one up and lifted it skywards. On the leg that shook in my hands, I saw the black number 51 on a blue ring. My shock was tinged with relief.

I placed Blue back down, checked the other remaining bird, then turned to face the carnage once again. Glimmers of light across the pool shone out with every colour of the rainbow. "My God, that's oil," I whispered. "My God . . . Tam," I thought, jumping to the obvious conclusion.

I felt really scared and wondered where he was. I considered for a moment whether to shout for help, and decided to make a run for the phone. But when I got to the office and dialled the number of the local SSPCA inspector who lived next door, his answering machine clicked on.

"Think now, think," I said to myself. The police . . . no . . . no good trying to explain this predicament. As the moments passed my fear and shock were joined by rage. "I'll kill him. He can't do that, no way." My mind raced. "He's too big to throttle . . ." I thought, and I looked about the office for some sort of weapon, to defend myself with or perhaps commit first-degree murder – I wasn't sure. Becoming a little more rational, I decided I'd have to find out where he was and play it cool until someone got back.

I ventured into the foyer again and could hear the clatter of the mop and bucket in the kitchen. Letting him get on with the job as if nothing had happened, I went to investigate. Quietly I moved Blue and his remaining companion to another area and collected up the bodies from the pool, realising with horror that the dead birds had literally had the life squeezed out of them. I felt sick as drips of blood fell into the water.

Where could he have got the oil? Walking back indoors, I spotted drips on the floor. I followed them down the corridor and outside. There were drips under the office window where I had seen Tam pass, and towards the utility shed beyond. There, in a dark corner by the rescue boat, I found a tray of used engine oil. A little had been recently spilled and there was a plastic cup with oil on it. The evidence kindled my rage again and foolishly I decided to confront him.

Calmly walking into the kitchen as if to make a coffee, I gave Tam a fright. He seemed very sheepish and would not look me in the eye. I walked slowly over to the sink where I could see a fish knife, and rested my back against the sink unit, facing him with folded arms.

"Well now, what have you been up to?" I said, deliberately.

"Nuh-hin," he said, smirking and plunging the mop into the bucket.

I felt like lunging at him.

"Really?" I said deliberately, staring him in the eye. Although scared of him physically, I knew he was not very bright.

I could not believe my eyes. There was blood everywhere, and iridescence swirling on the surface of the water was unmistakably oil.

"Wuznae me," he said, looking up briefly and smiling again. He said it as if he had said it a million times, it almost had a rhythm to it.

"What wuznae you, Tam?"

"Nah, I telt ye, nuh-hin," he said, looking confused and down at the floor.

"Really?" I said again slowly. My suspicions confirmed, I backed off and left him in the kitchen.

Now I felt strangely confident that I could remain alone with him in the building for a while and not suffer the same fate as the birds. He seemed too scared, not of me so much as my position as the one "in charge". Still, I anxiously awaited Sandra's return. By late that afternoon Tam had been officially relieved as a volunteer and by midnight that same evening part of the centre had been set on fire.

It was an incredible and shocking series of events. Although nobody was hurt and the wildlife we had at the time was unharmed by fire, it was only because the inspector, who lived on site, was woken by the sound of the flames that the entire centre was not destroyed. Only a barn used to house hay and other animal feeds, not animals themselves, was destroyed, but the fire still caused $50,000 worth of damage.

As the firemen sifted through the smouldering remains of a barn, we looked on in stunned silence and the police went in search of Tam. He was arrested that afternoon and would spend the next three years in jail. Only after his trial and conviction did we find out Tam was already a convicted arsonist.

The events cast a terrible cloud on the centre for days. Much of the camaraderie between the most recent volunteers and the regular crew, to which I fortunately belonged, was gone. Strict character assessments were put in place. For a while much of the humour that is so important during a crisis was absent, and we went about our business with quiet determination. For me, although I am still bitter and generally more cynical, it was an important lesson in life.

The anger I felt at the deaths of those birds was eased by the fact that Blue 51 had survived unharmed, although I kept my feelings to myself in the new atmosphere of cool professionalism. I was determined to be involved in Blue's release, having followed his fortunes so closely. He was for me like a symbol of recovery. And since he had been through so much and was the only bird currently ready and by now overdue for release, I suggested to Sandra that I let him go quietly and unannounced at St Andrews. She agreed. Our planned morale-boosting release, although

I was determined to be involved in Blue's release.

much needed, would now have to wait for a larger batch of birds once they were ready.

TWO DAYS AFTER THE FIRE, AND ON MY WAY HOME FOR A WEEKEND'S REST, I TOOK BLUE 51 WITH ME. I RELATED THE RECENT TERRIBLE EVENTS TO MY MOTHER, WHO HAD PICKED ME UP. BERRY, THE FAMILY DOG, SAT ON THE BACK SEAT, COMPLETELY ABSORBED BY THE SCENT OF BLUE IN HIS CARDBOARD BOX.

"You look exhausted. Couldn't you have chosen something simple like football as a hobby?" she said smiling.

Once we were home and unloaded I grabbed my binoculars and Blue's box and headed out the door. It was a cold and overcast morning, but the winds were slight and St Andrews Bay was calm. The moment had arrived and I savoured it. Before opening Blue's box I closed my eyes, breathed deep the fresh salty air and listened to the music of the sea. My mind filled with new images, no longer of individual birds but of hundreds, more than I could ever count, or save or draw, or singularly appreciate.

Blue's release was typical of a guillemot. For a moment he looked around, then was off like a shot, airborne once again and flying low to sea. A short distance away, he stopped and landed on the water and started preening fastidiously. I knew he would stay there for perhaps several hours, bathing and enjoying the sensation of his natural element again before taking off, flying low over the waves until he was no longer even a dot of black on the horizon. Seeing him go I was filled with joy and gratitude, and knew this was the completion of a particularly heart-wrenching and yet deeply rewarding cycle.

I realised I had now entered a very different phase of my life's passion. Through the centre and the oil spill I had now been exposed to the plight of wildlife beyond this beach – which had been my own little world, my own manageable battlefield – and experienced first hand a much bigger fight on a larger battlefield, a global war. And, as I whispered good luck and gave Blue his freedom, I felt happy and proud to have won Blue's battle. I was determined to march onwards towards other borders and other battles, armed with conviction and purpose – and, of course, the memory of Blue.

As far as I am aware, his metal ring has never been recovered.

His fate, therefore, remains in our imagination.

H E LOOKED AROUND AND THEN WAS OFF LIKE A SHOT, AIRBORNE ONCE AGAIN AND FLYING LOW OVER THE SEA UNTIL HE WAS NO LONGER EVEN A BLACK DOT ON THE HORIZON.

THE DORNOCH SPILL, IN MARCH 1987, ACCOUNTED FOR HUNDREDS OF AVIAN LIVES. ONLY THE PUBLIC PAID MORALLY OR FINANCIALLY FOR THE SPILL'S ENVIRONMENTAL DEVASTATION. THE ONLY TRUE PRICE PAID WAS THE LIVES OF WILD CREATURES AND THE EXHAUSTIVE EFFORTS OR MONETARY DONATIONS OF THOSE PEOPLE WHO VOLUNTEERED TO CARE FOR THEM. BY THE END OF MIDDLEBANK'S DORNOCH RESPONSE, WE HAD ACHIEVED ABOUT A 30 PERCENT SUCCESS RATE. CONSIDERING THE MANY FACTORS IN THAT PARTICULAR SPILL WE WERE CONTENT WITH OUR PERFORMANCE.

GIVEN THAT IT WAS ALSO OUR FIRST SPILL, WE HAD, I THOUGHT, DONE VERY WELL AND, MOST IMPORTANTLY, THE CENTRE HAD PROVED ITS IMMEDIATE VALUE AND WORTH TO THE SKEPTICS. WITH ALL THE ASSOCIATED PUBLICITY, THE CENTRE WAS NOW PLACED FIRMLY ON THE MAP AND ITS FUTURE SECURED. I FELT IT WAS NOW INEVITABLE THAT MIDDLEBANK WOULD EXPAND AND DEVELOP INTO A FULL-BLOWN WILDLIFE HOSPITAL, WHICH OF COURSE WOULD REQUIRE ADDITIONAL FULL TIME STAFF — AND, WITH LUCK, A PLACE FOR ME.

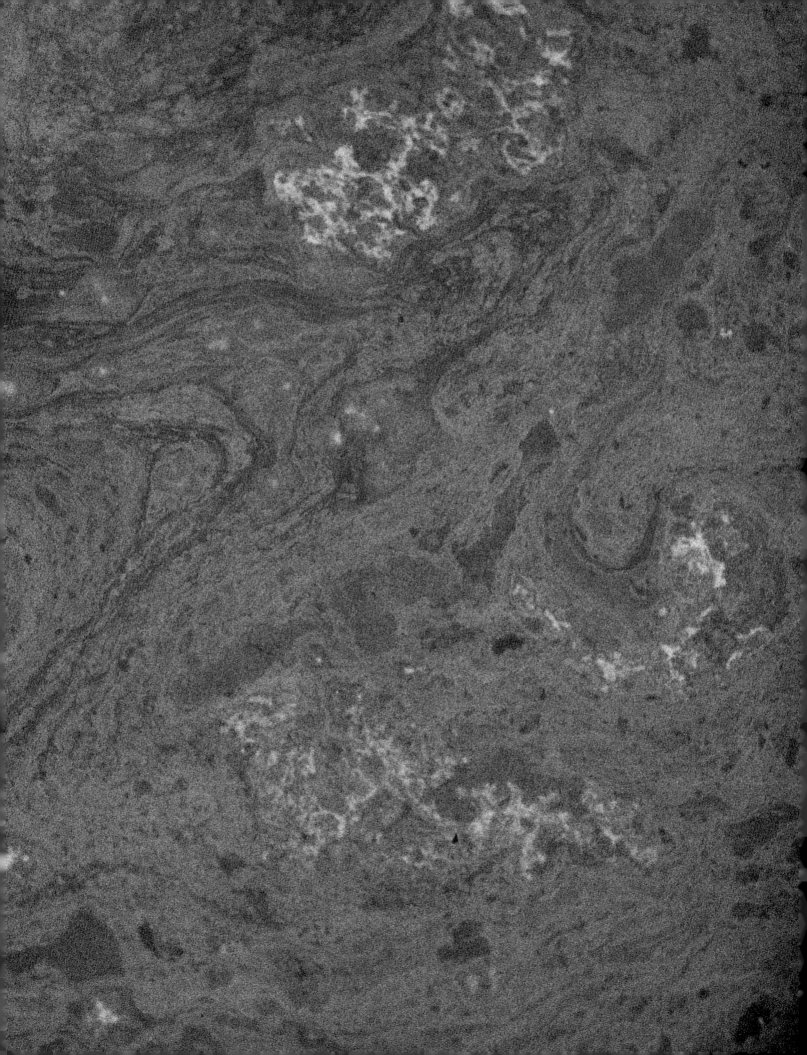

THE JEWEL

A KINGFISHER OUT OF THIS WORLD

THE JOVIAL VOICE ON MY ANSWERPHONE WAS UNMISTAKEABLE. IT WAS DON WILSON, THE SSPCA INSPECTOR FOR DUNDEE, AND I WAS IMMEDIATELY ON THE ALERT.

"So, you're out on a hot date, eh?" he joked. "Well, when you get in give me a call. I've got a really beautiful bird you'd love to see."

I collapsed into the one comfortable armchair in my Lilliputian flat and laughed, wondering how you could possibly describe yet another evening shift force feeding dead herrings to 20 bad-tempered seal pups as a "hot date". But Don knew that was the routine for us at Middlebank at this time of year. I had gone nine rounds wrestling those 20-kilogram babies, it was after 10 o'clock and I still hadn't had a proper meal. Dressed in dirty overalls and smelling awful, I knew the closest I'd get to a hot date that night was a pot of fresh tea.

But just hearing Don's voice made me grin. He was a naturally humorous man and I always enjoyed making contact with him. I phoned Don back straight away, excited but wary. He was infamous for practical jokes and this had all the signs. But I'd missed him and got his answerphone. Don worked from home, so I guessed he was out on call. I scrubbed up and got myself to bed, knowing it would be yet another long day wrestling baby seals tomorrow.

It was March, and in early springtime the centre was overflowing, with small creatures tucked into every available corner. In the morning, between mucking out the hedgehogs and the first seal feed, curiosity got the better of me and I put in my call. To my surprise Don's message turned out to be no practical joke. He was brief and to the point: he did have a bird I would love to see, a bird that was both rare and undoubtedly one of Europe's most beautiful. My heart started to race. I knew immediately which lovely bird he was talking about – a kingfisher. It was like winning the lottery. I had only ever heard of one kingfisher brought into a rehabilitation centre before. And now we were going to be given one to look after.

As soon as I could I was on my way to Dundee in the SSPCA van, humming with excitement and anticipation and alive to all the joys of the world. But as I thought about the situation a bit more, I started to come down to earth. Previous experience told me that any bird that came to us at Middlebank, and particularly a bird as notoriously elusive as the kingfisher, was likely to be in a bit of a state. "It'll be all manky," I told myself, like a kid not wanting to get their hopes up but hoping nevertheless. "It'll be injured, I'm bound to be disappointed."

And yet Don had said the bird was in good condition and he was at a loss regarding its problem. "Perhaps it wasn't serious?" I allowed myself to wonder.

As I drove the 70 kilometres north I was also thinking about the last time I had seen a wild kingfisher. Growing up in Scotland by the coast did not offer much opportunity to see these rare and wonderful birds, and although I had heard of sightings in the county, these were often well beyond the range of my bike. Members of my bird club had spotted a pair living on the river about 15 kilometres away from St Andrews, and as a teenager I had tried unsuccessfully to find them. I had even organised lifts with friends who were in the enviable possession of wheels with a combustion engine and not pedals, but the expeditions had always proved fruitless.

I had to wait till I was 21 and a student at art school in Wales before I saw my first and only kingfisher, and it was no more than a fleeting glimpse, a flash of iridescent blue plumage darting down a river, fast and low across the water. To see a kingfisher at rest is even more unusual.

They are generally scarce now in the United Kingdom, for the usual reasons – pollution and loss of habitat. To me, the kingfisher somehow doesn't seem to belong in the soft and muted colours of the British

Opposite: Sometimes you know when you've got a great photograph, and it seemed that every frame I shot was a gem. I would probably never have an opportunity like this again.

A KINGFISHER'S GLITTERING AND COLOURFUL PLUMAGE IS A LIKE A FLASH OF THE TROPICS AGAINST THE SOFT BRITISH LANDSCAPE.

landscape. Its brightness and iridescence, the particular way it seems to hold or refract the sunlight, seem to belong more with the brilliance of the tropics.

Because of their brilliant colouring they have, deservedly, been described by many, whether in poetry or conversation, as the jewels of the riverbank. As I sat that night with an immaculate young female kingfisher perched on my finger only inches away, I felt I was in possession of something more beautiful and more precious than any jewel.

In the excitement, I hadn't quizzed Don for details about how the kingfisher came into his possession. I had a quick peek in the carton, knowing that a kingfisher would probably try to escape. This tiny bird just sat there, absolutely immaculate and without any visible sign of injury or distress. It was incredible. I should have known then and there what was wrong with it. Her immediate appearance and behaviour were most perplexing. Back at the centre I had examined her carefully. Because of the orange on the lower mandible of the beak I knew she was female. No more than 10 centimetres long including the tail, she fitted easily in the palm on my hand. Because of her fragility, her glittering iridescence, and my excitement, I held her nervously, like some stolen diamond that would never be mine. But there were no obvious breaks or apparent damage, no wounds or broken feathers.

For a bird so secretive and wary of human beings, and which adjusts so poorly to captivity, it seemed incredible that she perched so happily on my finger. A distressed bird will pant and try to escape, dart around, hurl itself at anything in its way. It's not a pretty sight, and to stop them bashing and damaging themselves further you've got to keep them in enclosed cardboard boxes. But she just sat there, not visibly distressed and making no attempt to move.

It was an irresistible opportunity to take some photographs. I knew that if I was to work in wildlife rehabilitation for the rest of my life in the United Kingdom I would probably never have this opportunity again. People have taken amazing photos of kingfishers in the wild in recent years, but only after exhaustive hours of patient observation and preparation and with the highly sophisticated equipment necessary to catch their high-speed flight, equipment that was well beyond my budget. It was an extraordinary stroke of luck to have one so close and at rest, not darting and diving after fish.

She sat like the perfect model as I set up my camera, making no attempt to fly away. Since it was dark outside I would have to use a flash. I was nervous about that because wildlife, already terrified by human contact, often do not take kindly to sudden flashes of blinding light.

Not so this subject. She seemed a little nervous about the click of the shutter, but there was so little reaction to the flashing light . . . . I stopped, struck by a sudden thought. I took her up on my fingers once more and put the room light on. I looked closely into one eye then switched the light off and on again.

"Damn," I thought, "she's blind!"

The lack of pupillary response explained it all. Like a human eye, a bird's pupil will close down in bright light and open in low light. Hers did not change at all.

I felt intensely sad, knowing deep inside that her case was probably hopeless. The next 24 hours would seal her fate, and I knew that if she didn't see after that time her chances of recovery were slim. Photographing her became even more poignant, knowing that she would not be with us for long.

Because she showed no sign of distress, I kept photographing. It was an amazing hour and a half and I took several rolls of film. Sometimes you know when you've got a great photograph, and it seemed that every frame I shot was a gem. It was like spoiling myself, and I couldn't wait to see them.

But I was also worried about the kingfisher. I supposed her blindness was caused by neurological damage, maybe caused by some sort of impact injury to her head or spine. Whatever had happened it was recent, because she was still in immaculate condition.

As with knocks to the human head, the damage can be either temporary concussion or permanent, and I feared the worst. Our policy was to give a creature with such injuries an injection to reduce inflammation, bruising or swelling of the nerves in the hope that some normal functioning would return. With a bigger bird like a swan you can inject into the thigh muscle, but with such tiny birds I usually injected into the muscle of the breast, which is backed by a bony plate or keel that protects internal organs.

There was nothing else I could do. I put her on a towel in a dark warm place to rest for the night. Twenty-four hours passed with no change. She showed no interest in food and her condition was deteriorating. A kingfisher in the wild is a fishing bird, and in captivity they very rarely want to eat at all, especially not the dead fish we could offer. The only other option is to force feed them, and they don't take kindly to that. Before you know it you've got a bird that's so distressed it is sometimes not worth trying. I was loath to even attempt feeding her because I knew that it was just delaying the inevitable. I think the moment I saw she was blind I realised there was no way to rehabilitate her.

There are always ethical and moral considerations in deciding when to end another creature's life. Some people believe we play God by not going to any lengths to save a creature's life. But I believe that putting a blind kingfisher or a one-winged guillemot into an aviary is equally playing God. I always keep in mind what life a creature has in the wild where it belongs, and how much that would be compromised by captivity. There was, sadly, no way this kingfisher would survive, and her plumage started to suggest that. It seemed to lose its iridescence, and within two days the colours dulled and the feathers became messy because she wasn't preening. She was fading away before our eyes. It became painfully obvious that our jewel of the riverbank was dying.

It was only a matter of checking with Sandra Hogben, the centre manager, and getting a second opinion before making the decision we were both loath to make. We held off for a couple of days. Then, during an attempt to force feed her that was doing more harm than good, we decided to end her suffering.

Holding her gently in my hands I inserted the needle and slowly injected.

In a second and without resistance her small colourful body sagged, her head dropped and the precious jewel left our possession. It had been a brief and wonderful encounter, and the photographs I took are a tribute to her memory and beauty.

BOTTLE

THE HERON FROM HELL

A FRANTIC WOMAN ON THE END ON THE PHONE SAID SHE HAD A STRANGE-LOOKING CHICK WITH A LONG NECK. IT LOOKED RIDICULOUS, SHE SAID, AND IT HAD A FUNNY HAIRCUT. IT COULD ONLY BE ONE THING, I THOUGHT, A BABY HERON.

Wildlife turns up at a wildlife rehabilitation centre in the most outrageous variations of carrying cases and boxes. This time I was presented with a gold and black Benson and Hedges cigarette carton. By the expressions on the faces of the couple presenting it to me, it was obvious they believed that the current occupant, rather than the cigarettes, warranted a government health warning.

I took the box into the reception room and carefully opened the lid, just enough to see what was inside. It was the only time I can recall being actually filled with delight at the contents. (Usually they turn up so mangled or distressed the sight is not a pretty one.)

Λ scrawny head poked out. Two bright daffodil-yellow eyes stared up at me from under the most bizarre haircut I'd ever seen. It was a hilarious and surreal sight, this wildly unconventional head poking out of a cardboard cigarette box, looking around with a wide-eyed expression of intense

It looked as if the current occupant rather than the cigarettes might warrant a government health warning, but for me it was love at first sight.

curiosity. Depending on what he saw, the baby heron's crest of fledgling down rose up and down like a punk rocker's pompadour.

"Well, look at you," I said. "You look like you've stuck your fingers in a light socket!"

For me, it was love at first sight. Without opposition I was able to gather him up and place him on a towel for closer inspection. He was about four weeks old, and already about 50 centimetres high. At that age, before their wings are fully formed, heron chicks will often lean forward on their "knees" – the leg joint about 15 centimetres off the ground.

The creature's bulbous stomach extended up into his neck, and when he stood up, his legs were only half of adult proportions, so it looked as if his stomach was supporting all his weight. With his long neck sprouting from this extended body, the heron chick looked exactly like a little bottle with legs. And so he would be christened, Bottle.

The couple who had brought him to the Middlebank wildlife rescue centre were very anxious about the alien that had landed in their lives, and even more curious to know what it was. They knew it was a bird, obviously, but it took some explaining to convince them it wasn't prehistoric.

They had been out walking in a forest when their Alsatian dog sniffed out a solitary heron nest that may have blown down in a gale. Before they could stop him, the dog had destroyed one of the nest's two chicks. I realised that, in fact, if the dog hadn't smelled them out both chicks would probably have died anyway.

The couple had driven about 150 kilometres up from the border of Scotland to bring the survivor to the centre, having tried, unsuccessfully, to feed the chick on bread and milk for almost a week. Almost everybody who rescues a creature of any kind tries to do this, but it is probably the worst thing you can give to most wildlife. It was a wonder this young bird was still living.

I was on duty at the centre on my own that day. Thankfully it was quiet, but that was an exception. Springtime, when many young creatures are born, was a busy time of year at Middlebank, with baby hedgehogs, many fledgling birds, ducklings, and sometimes grey seals in residence.

I quickly returned to the box and its contents. With a fixed stare the creature looked at me and croaked loudly. The noise was something like the sound of ripping cardboard, a sort of KRAARK, and it meant one thing only – "FEED ME".

Bottle was lively and not suffering too badly from stress, but it was obvious he needed nourishment. Feeding any young bird is a difficult and

Bottle, like all young herons, would sit supporting all his weight on his stomach, which made him look somewhat comical.

Opposite: As a chick he looked decidedly prehistoric.

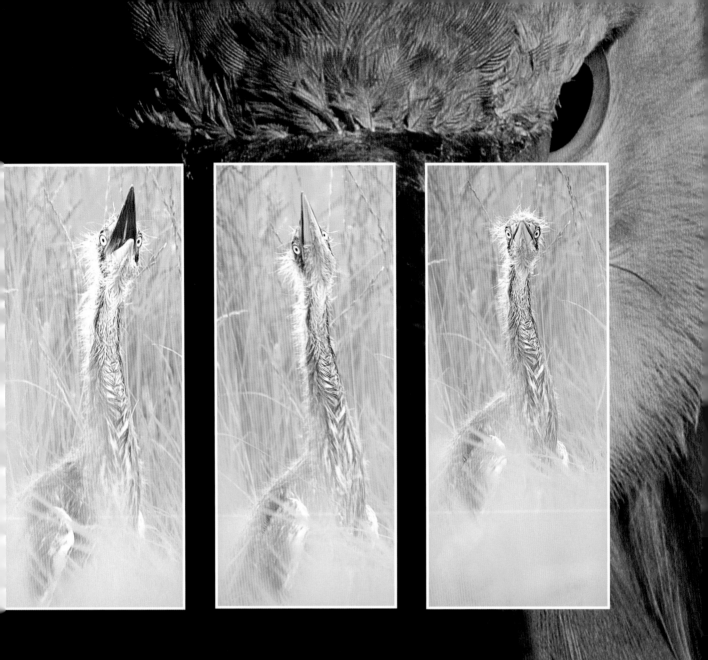

The second time I photographed Bottle he had been at Middlebank wildlife rescue centre for about a week and his plumage was still fairly respectable.

I took Bottle outside into a field, put him down on the grass and started clicking expression after expression. It was hilarious. He'd fix on a worm or an ant and his gaze would follow it intently as if he couldn't believe what he was seeing. He was like a baby, or a visionary, seeing the world with fresh eyes. Suddenly he'd lose interest and look at me again, as if to say "Okay, your call, what's next?".

When an aircraft flew overhead, he looked at it in amazement, wondering, I suppose, what type of creature it was and whether it was some distant relative. Then he looked back at me, yawned, preened and picked at something minute in the grass. Like any kid or young animal he had the attention span of a gnat.

delicate business, and very few birds survive. Supplying the correct diet is essential if the bird is to grow and develop properly, and this is never easy. Neither is meeting the voracious demand. In the wild parent birds will happily devote all their time to the pursuit and collection of adequate and various food items.

Adult herons, like other aquatic birds, catch and swallow their prey first before returning to the nest to feed their offspring. On arrival there follows a feeding procedure that is amazingly efficient and effective and is executed with very little mess.

The baby herons jostle to receive the contents of the parents' stomachs, mouth to mouth, like eager waste disposal units. In this way a wholesome meal can be delivered in a few seconds. Regurgitation worked beautifully in the wild, but how were we to feed our resident punk rocker?

Our first line of attack was a liquidised fish mix, similar to that used to rear seals, delivered by a syringe. The first feed would very quickly determine how successful this would be, and be decisive in how well the chick would respond to further hand feeding.

My first dinner date with Bottle was an unmitigated disaster, a truly unromantic affair. He hated being picked up and his little legs shot out in all directions. I managed to squirt the contents of the syringe into Bottle's throat, only for him to look at me with contempt, turn his head and regurgitate with an expressive "bluurrhhh" over his shoulder. This was just the beginning.

Next time, for variation, he shook his head while he vomited, spraying fish mix in all directions and achieving nothing other than an unsavoury redecoration of the reception room. I sat, looking at Bottle in despair, amidst wall-to-wall fish mix. Bottle sat looking defiant but no less comical. The look meant only one thing – DIFFICULT CHILD.

I retired gracefully and returned to the office to report progress to Sandra, who had turned up by this stage and was curious about the new arrival. This was a brief report, delivered in few words – which I'm sure suited Sandra perfectly, given the atrocious smell of my clothing.

Our resident punk rocker had an amazingly theatrical range of expressions.

But if Bottle were to survive – let alone thrive – he had to be fed, so we had to persevere. With so much food passing through him, I suspected he must be keeping at least some of it down, so I was confident I had given him at least some nourishment.

The battles continued but, with the help of a specially adapted stomach tube fitted to the end of the syringe, mealtimes with Bottle became a little easier and began, to a degree, to achieve their goal. Because Bottle kept so little food down, it was a matter of giving him frequent feeds, up to nine times a day. We all found it hard to believe how our Bottle remained upright. He was desperately thin but not short of spirit, sometimes annoyed by us but always full of fun. He was truly a bird of character.

It is a tribute to nature that the parental feeding method is achieved with so little mess. Although an infant heron's dress sense could hardly be described as tidy, while in the nest they manage to keep their feathers clean, having quickly learned from their parents how to preen. The process is essential for any bird, but especially for aquatic birds, if they are to remain waterproof and keep their feathers in good condition for flight. With a young bird it's even more important because in that first year they will have to learn to fly.

Unfortunately Bottle didn't have a clue about personal cleanliness and hygiene. This wasn't surprising, given the totally alien environment in which he was growing up. I wasn't setting a particularly good example. I must confess to turning up on a number of our early morning breakfast dates and being confronted with a creature that bore an amazing resemblance to the one I'd seen in the mirror a short time before.

Within a few days Bottle was an absolute mess – slimy, crusty and stinky. But somehow that just added to his character. His head was mostly out of regurgitation range, so Bottle's crowning glory was still clean enough for him to raise it up and down, emphasising every triumph and every one of his amazingly theatrical range of expressions.

It was time for Bottle to have a bath. We were quite used to bathing birds, but for Bottle it was a different story. Amidst a cloud of steam and soap suds, Bottle was most indignant and made his feelings known to all inside the wash room and, I might add, a few kilometres beyond.

That night he demonstrated another of his many traits, his sense of timing and capacity for revenge. After what appeared to be a very successful feeding session he sat and stared at me then took great delight in vomiting all over himself. He had won the day and that particular battle, but the war was not over. Whether he liked it or not the words "Bottle – bath" in the diary became a regular feature.

A S SUMMER UNFOLDED AND WITH NUMEROUS OTHER YOUNG MOUTHS FOR US TO FEED, BOTTLE SOON FOUND HIMSELF IN THE BACKGROUND OF CURRENT AFFAIRS. IF WE HAD TO CREATE MORE SPACE, IT WAS USUALLY BOTTLE WHO HAD TO MOVE HOUSE AND HE DID SO HAPPILY, RELISHING ANY NEW SURROUNDINGS.

In the wild, adult herons are generally very shy, and it would be unusual to hear their croaking call. But Bottle was quite vocal, constantly making noises, calling out and croaking.

Although desperately thin, Bottle was still lively, full of fun and unusually vocal for a heron.

Opposite: Bottle didn't have a clue about personal cleanliness. After the battles of force feeding he was an absolute mess — slimy, crusty and stinky.

Of the many thousands of birds that came through Middlebank, it was Bottle I remember most clearly. He was unforgettable. As a result it wasn't long before he had developed his own fan club. Everyone loved him. He was never short of visitors from the staff and from the organised groups of adults or children who came almost daily to Middlebank.

Bottle loved children, which was a distinct contrast to his reaction to adults. When adults were invited to view him he would just sit indignantly staring as you discussed his plight. If you were lucky, his expression might change, perhaps in fear and anticipation of syringes and stomach tubes. But children were exciting and made lots of noise and so did he.

As soon as he heard their voices he would jump off his perch at the back of the aviary, his crest going up and down like a fan opening and closing, and strut up to wait at the aviary door. There, under the gaze of excited, giggling children, he would go into his extrovert dance, rear end up in the air, flapping his wings, strutting and croaking like an avian Mick Jagger.

In front of children, Bottle would begin an extrovert dance, strutting and wiggling his backside like an avian Mick Jagger.

Almost every return post from school visits during Bottle's residence brought with it hilarious pictures and descriptions of his performance, and it was clear he would not be easily forgotten. He became a very effective educational tool and an important asset in getting our message across about respecting wildlife, but we had no desire to keep him or make him into a pet. As with any wild creature that came our way our sole intention remained his successful return to the wild. Bottle, sadly, was still a long way from that.

Although he could now fly there remained his personal hygiene problems, and of more concern was the fact that he was still not apparently feeding on his own. Other young animals will reject anything you give them as a way of showing they just don't like you. If they can't bite you they'll throw up instead. But if they are going to survive, they sooner rather than later learn that the experience of being fed by humans results in a nice full stomach.

Herons will naturally disgorge food when alarmed, so we were in a difficult position right from the start. Bottle never stopped regurgitating, usually all over himself and quite deliberately. Unlike other animals, there was never that moment of understanding when he finally accepted handling and feeding. I'd walk away, pleased with myself and thinking I had a syringe of food down him, and five minutes later come back to find it all spewed up in the corner.

You'd think that a bird doing that would be an unhappy wee soul and a lot of the birds we got in were like that. With Bottle it was more like "Oh hell, here they go again", and when it was over he'd vomit and resume his usual bright-eyed perkiness. But he was pitifully thin and his keel – the bony ridge down his front – was standing out. That was a real worry. Birds in such bad condition are likely to go out like a light, and that was always my concern with Bottle.

We had tried every conceivable method of persuasion with an assortment of fish of different sizes and presentations – herrings, sprats, whole and pulverised, various feeding trays, different scenery, even at the pools – but nothing made the slightest difference. It was very frustrating to watch him showing more interest in sticks and feathers than fish.

I remember on one of my rare days off, after a successful first attempt at trout fishing, I stood in my kitchen proudly examining my catch and deciding how to cook it when Bottle sprang to mind.

Before long my noble offering lay at Bottle's feet. He looked at it, then looked at me, decided it made a lovely perch, stood on it, ignoring my prize catch, and pushed at the sticks and leaves on the ground.

My patience exhausted, I sat down in his enclosure and began delivering a stern and fatherly chat. Bottle, by that stage, had achieved nearly one metre adult height although nothing like the mature heron's one-and-a-half-metre wing span or its weight.

Still standing on the fish he looked at me with interest, obviously wondering where the noise I was making came from. Staring fixedly at my mouth, he strutted towards me. I was a little apprehensive as to his intentions. Bottle had never shown any sign of aggression, his complaints up till now were all vocal. But a heron's very sharp, long beak is designed for hunting and spearing fish, and the first thing a normal adult heron will do is go for your eyes.

I kept on talking. He looked very exited and, offering a throaty croak, attempted to put his beak into my mouth. Finding it impossible not to laugh, I turned my head away and he quickly lost interest and returned to his fishy perch.

"I know what your trying to tell me," I chortled, "I should have eaten it first. There are some things I won't do Bottle, and that's one of them."

But despite his obvious and outward reluctance to feed himself we did come to the conclusion Bottle must have fed on occasion. The amount of force-fed fish he was given daily was not enough to maintain his weight, yet he did, although he wasn't really gaining weight.

Had he not been a bird, I'd have put his behaviour down to sheer spite.

Then one morning on my arrival at work I was confronted with a message in large capitals on the daily chores blackboard. On it I read with delight that Bottle had eaten a fish, by himself.

Bottle seemed to take more interest in sticks and stones than in our offerings. We were in despair.

These momentous words on the staff blackboard confronted me one memorable day. There was no looking back. I delighted in just watching him eat.

What clicked I don't know. But at that moment I knew Bottle was going to survive.

Perhaps Bottle had at last decided it was time to leave the nest. This historic day had come after nearly five months of force feeding. Other young birds were in and out of the centre in a matter of weeks. But it was nearly a year before Bottle left us.

We had to wait while Bottle put on weight. But after this breakthrough there was no looking back. Daily he would demolish a generous supply of fish like a bird possessed. I took great delight in taking him a tray of fish and watching him bolt it down. It was wonderful to just watch him eat. But his appearance was still a total disgrace, and he smelt awful.

THE PROBLEM NOW WAS TO DO SOMETHING ABOUT HIS IMPRINTING – THE WAY HE HAD MODELLED HIMSELF ON HUMANS RATHER THAN HIS OWN KIND. IN THE BACK OF ALL OUR MINDS THERE WAS ONE QUESTION: "HOW ON EARTH DO WE RELEASE THIS BIRD?"

Despite the fact Bottle could fly perfectly well and was by now eating on his own, we remained very sceptical about letting him go directly into the wild. He had been with us now almost a year and was hopelessly imprinted, treating humans as a source of food rather than a threat. This fact alone would mean almost certain death if he was merely allowed to fly away. He was far too friendly and would actively seek people.

This was put to the test one awful morning. We were having a well-earned coffee break one day when, to my horror, I noticed Bottle at the top of the chestnut tree outside the office. Every now and then a bird did escape and when that happened usually we'd lost our bird for good because there was simply no way to catch it again.

We were appalled at the idea of Bottle flying off, which would have been an absolute disaster for him. He sat on top of the chestnut tree, making his usual croaking "arrrk, arrrrk" call. We rushed out, hoping to lure him down from his vantage point. We must have looked quite ridiculous, but we had urgent business to attend to. Staff and volunteers circled the tree, making a range of heron-type noises, tempting him with fish, trying anything that might attract Bottle back down, all of us feeling slightly frantic and yet trying to present a calm exterior.

Bottle, unimpressed, stayed exactly where he was. He continued looking down at us with his characteristic ironic stare, all the time krawwing and kraaking, crest fanning up and down as if he was thumbing his nose at us.

He spent at least half a day up the tree, and I swear he was laughing at us. We couldn't take our eyes off him for a minute in case he disappeared, so the business of the centre was completely disrupted. He finally took off and our hearts were racing madly. To our great relief, he landed in the field just long enough for one of the inspectors to execute a spectacular flying rugby tackle and grab Bottle as he spread his wings for the great blue yonder. Once again, it was with a mixture of frustration and relief that we settled our long-term resident back in care.

It was even more clear to us that we had to find him some sort of relocation rather than release, somewhere that provided a sense of freedom but still under the watchful eye of human allies.

With much thought and investigation we found Palaceriggs Country Park. It is situated in a rural setting in the central lowlands near the city of Glasgow and as well as providing the usual park facilities and ample space it boasts a small collection of aquatic birds in an open enclosure. Most importantly it had a staff of wildlife-minded rangers who were quite willing to keep a watchful eye on our young delinquent heron.

Above, below and overleaf: Playing truant from Middlebank one evening, Bottle and I visited a nearby poppy field, where he proved the perfect photographic subject.

Since the enclosure was open, Bottle would for the first two or three weeks be introduced to his new setting from a makeshift enclosed aviary. Merely placing him in the open enclosure and letting him get on with it would most probably result in chaos, not only for its established residents, but with the park's human visitors.

Sadly, on the day Bottle left for his new home I was on holiday, and on my return things were just not the same. I missed him, and felt strangely sad. Over the years I had been involved with many creatures and quite deliberately, assisted by the sheer numbers at any one time, I'd managed not to get too attached. But Bottle would always be special   his plight had been so demanding, his character so enchanting. It was an encounter never to be forgotten.

In his absence we could only satisfy ourselves with regular inquiries about his progress, which was, so far, very good. He was now out among other birds and by all accounts happily finding a niche of his own.

Now he was almost fully grown it was time for Bottle to find another home.

SIX MONTHS LATER, DURING A VERY LOW SPOT WHEN DEATHS AT THE CENTRE FAR OUTWEIGHED THE SUCCESSES, I SAT IN MY MINIATURE FLAT IN THE PICTURESQUE VILLAGE OF LIMEKILNS ON A DAY OFF, WONDERING HOW I MIGHT CHEER MYSELF UP. MY EYE WAS DRAWN TO A PHOTOGRAPH ON MY WALL OF BOTTLE GAZING COMICALLY AT AN AIRCRAFT PASSING OVERHEAD.

"Visit Bottle," I thought, but I felt sceptical. Supposing he had disappeared or, worse still, was dead? It might make me feel even more depressed. These thoughts preyed on my mind as I drove through the dead and colourless winter countryside on the way to Palaceriggs Park.

Very rarely do you have the opportunity to see again the wildlife you've released. This was one of the very few times I was able to do that. Bottle, although he could fly and had his freedom if he wanted to, had chosen to stay within the confines of the park as far as I knew.

The enclosure was signposted and easy to find. From a distance I could see four very large storks sitting hunched up against the cold. As I got closer, I spotted a smaller bird amongst them. It was a grey heron.

Gripping the fence with excitement, I took a closer look. "It couldn't be," I thought, "He's too tidy."

In front of me stood the smartest grey heron I had ever seen. If it was Bottle, he had somehow learned the art of keeping clean. I really wasn't sure. The bird was proud, his beautiful, full adult plumage in immaculate condition, with long, long legs and only the slightest remains of a crest.

As he was now a young adult, Bottle's crest of down was beginning to diminish.

The bird suddenly raised his head and looked towards a small group of children who were beside the fence shouting and giggling at the statuesque storks. With interest the heron moved off towards them, proudly strutting like a king.

"It is, it must be Bottle." My heart was pounding with excitement. In the heron's way stood one of the storks, and it was a good three times his size. With a croak and a sharp head butt, Bottle sent it packing. "That's true to form," I thought, smiling proudly.

As he stood by the fence I walked around to get closer and find out if the recognition was mutual. I would be so happy if it was. But I looked at him and he looked at me and he showed no sign of recognising me at all.

I remembered how I would always imitate his croaking, throaty call if we were alone, to which he often answered. So, making sure no one was in ear shot, I gave it my best try. Other than a slight tilt of his head there was nothing, no response.

After a few quiet words I stood up and started walking away. As I did so, I heard a familiar croak, a voice that could only be Bottle's. It was recognition enough.

I have never returned to Palaceriggs, nor have I phoned. For me, somehow, I wanted our encounter to end there.

With dusk descending, I said farewell to Bottle. But he would retain a special place in my heart and remain one of my strongest memories of wildlife rescue.

Opposite page: In front of me stood the smartest grey heron I had ever seen.

LUCKY

IS A FAT GOOSE NERVOUS IN DECEMBER?

This goose was not supposed to see out the year, and was clearly intended for a large serving platter.

CHRISTMASTIME AT MIDDLEBANK OFFERED NO REPRIEVE FROM THE DAILY ROUND OF MUCKING OUT ENCLOSURES AND FORCING DEAD HERRINGS DOWN THE GULLETS OF BAD–TEMPERED SEAL PUPS.

In some ways it was an even harder time of year for me. The weather in south-west Fife in the depths of winter was relentlessly miserable. It was dark by half past three in the afternoon, and what little daylight we got was grey, cold, wet and overcast. The centre had to be staffed 365 days of the year, and over the holiday season that meant either centre manager Sandra Hogben or I had to be on duty. Volunteers were thin on the ground, caught up in family celebrations or away (sensibly) on holiday. Because I preferred to throw myself into the festivities of New Year, I opted to be on duty Christmas Day, which was usually a fairly strange and lonely experience.

I was always short of money, but I'd take a bottle of wine and drink it with the seals in the icy barn, telling them about my disappointments of the year past and hopes for the year to come. Their total disregard, as they

Opposite: Geese make a raucous trumpeting sound that I'm quite sure the entire wind section of the London Philharmonic could not reproduce.

Lucky pulled no punches. He constantly taunted everyone and everything, even what seemed to me to be empty space. His head shot forward and he hissed, "Come on then . . . tak ye noo," like a Highland "bovver boy".

blearily closed their eyes, yawned, scratched and farted, brought me thoroughly down to earth. Then, in the evening, I'd go to Glasgow for a family meal and hot whiskies which, by that stage, I really needed.

The rest of the day passed going into battle to force feed aggressive grey seal pups, each determined to sink its teeth into my most vulnerable and private parts. Seals were breeding and giving birth in November and December, and we received many pups which had been abandoned on the more public beaches because of human disturbance. They were often out of condition and covered with wounds inflicted by other seals or gulls. But once they recovered their fighting spirit they made it clear they were not happy about the accommodation, the menu or the service.

We usually also had a full complement of overwintering hedgehogs and adult birds battered by or struggling against the inclement weather. So just before the Christmas of 1991 I greeted with pleasure the arrival of a defiant character, a domestic goose, who lightened my mood and provided welcome relief from the stresses of the year's end. This deliciously plump and fighting-fit bird reminded me of the old saying when stating the obvious, "Is a fat goose nervous in December?" Any sensible goose would have been more nervous than this one.

We'd received a call from a woman near the fishing village of Anstruther on what is called the East Neuk (East Corner) of Fife. She had encountered the bird, which was announcing itself in no uncertain terms, on the driveway of her farm. It proved to be not so much an encounter as a stand-off. The goose stood its ground against the farmer's on-coming vehicle and made it quite clear it was prepared to enter into a physical confrontation.

Geese challenge the very term "domestic" and can be fearless creatures, completely confident in their aggression and willing to take on the world if they feel it's necessary, which they seem to do quite often. As a result they are sometimes used as guards to protect property. Their fighting spirit is often enough to deter the hardiest of thieves. One famous group of geese is entrusted to protect the warehouse of the company which produces one of Scotland's most precious assets – whisky.

Many people are equally frightened of swans, which fluff up their feathers and can give you a good whack with their wings. But geese seem to make a better job of being aggressive. Their heads and long necks shoot forward as they make a run at you, their eyes pop out and their sturdy beaks are capable of giving you a good peck. But it's their noise which is so effective.

Geese make a raucous trumpeting sound which the entire wind section of the London Philharmonic could not reproduce. It's the only thing I can imagine that must be more frightening than a very hairy Scotsman in a kilt

running at you with a two-metre claymore, yelling "freedom" to the sound of bagpipes. Like badly played bagpipes, this trumpeting has the effect of paralysing the victim before the attack, that is, after the victim has emptied his or her bladder. Then, hissing and with open stretched wings, the goose charges.

It's a bit like the battle of Bannockburn, all you can do is run away, unless you happen to have a loaf of bread in your pocket. Then geese will happily negotiate a ceasefire. In this case, the farmer was used to handling stroppy stock, and she managed to restrain the goose, put it aside in a cage and call Middlebank. There were stories about Middlebank in the local paper once every couple of weeks, and many Fife people were aware there was a wildlife rescue centre. The goose, although fiery tempered, was not strictly wild, but we were used to getting all sorts of referrals.

Luckily for the bird we were not long in arriving, for it suddenly dawned on the woman that the goose was almost certainly an escapee from a neighbouring farm, and that if she had started asking around the neighbourhood she would have found no shortage of owners. This goose was not supposed to see out the year, and was clearly intended for a large serving platter. We managed to negotiate its reprieve and the woman promised to pretend the encounter never occurred. For the neighbouring farmer it would be a case of "goose missing, presumed lucky".

Whether it's swans or geese getting a bit aggressive, you've got to show them who's boss. The first thing is to get their wings under control, which requires a lot of strength. The way to do this is to go for the base of the

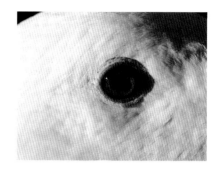

Blue-eyed beauties, but without the personality to match.

Opposite and left: Between bouts of aggression, Lucky would turn his attention to fastidious preening of his feathers.

neck, pin them to the ground so they are not able to stand up, then put an arm around wings and body, tucking them under your arm back to front like a rugby ball or a set of feathery white bagpipes, so that if you have to go through doors they won't smack their heads.

The way to transport large birds which are too big for a box is to put them head first into a fertiliser sack with one corner cut off, then tie up the bottom of the bag like a straitjacket. This way they can't stand up or flap their wings and all they can really do is look around. This was the procedure with the errant goose. As I bundled the fortunate creature in the van it looked at me and the woman and hissed loudly in ungrateful defiance. "Aye," I said, "If only you knew, mate."

For the remainder of the journey to the centre our proud, fat Christmas goose – by now christened what else but "Lucky" – sat looking out the back window and hissing at anything that moved. Considering we were in perpetual motion, this meant a constant stream of what could only be described as abuse from the back seat. Everything seemed to piss him off.

Out of sight but most certainly not out of sound, Lucky spent his Christmas at the centre and clearly felt justified in pronouncing himself boss when anyone so much as looked at him. We couldn't help but admire his arrogance and liked him because he was so stroppy. Here we were doing the creature a massive favour and all we got was constant aggression.

When the festive season was over we started to search for a safe haven for Lucky. This search was greatly accelerated after an untimely encounter between Lucky and a visiting SSPCA executive. Lucky took an instant and

intense dislike to the poor man, behaving as if the executive had no business on the premises whatsoever. At least the business – mostly accounts and number crunching – was over and the executive was returning to his vehicle when Lucky struck. As a head office man, he was always impeccably dressed in suit and tie, and showed no interest in staying for any hands-on experience of Middlebank.

We'd got used to having Lucky around the centre and we would let him out to graze underneath the chestnut tree. I could only watch helplessly as Lucky spotted the suit and shot across the yard, his chest puffed out like a Dunfermline lout hissing, "Eh, big man, come on then, take yae now."

Luckily for all of us, the goose failed to make contact. Somewhere between the trumpeting and the charge, the executive was in his car, flailing about in his rush to close the windows. I found it hard to stop myself laughing as the poor man sped out of the yard, tyres screeching. After that event, despite a generally amicable relationship with headquarters, I did sometimes wish I were a goose.

Lucky is now residing on, or should I perhaps say ruling, a farm in central Scotland. We managed to locate one of those happy places where, alongside the everyday running of the farm, the owners enjoyed being surrounded by all sorts of animals which they treated as companions and not food items. It was our hope that this lucky goose would see out his fair share of Christmas Days there.

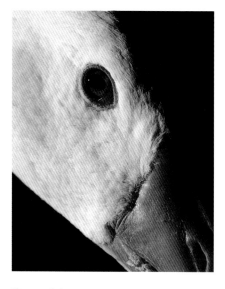

Everything seemed to annoy him. Gratitude was not Lucky's strong suit.

Lucky made few friends at Middlebank – with his attitude that was hardly surprising.

ALBA

A PEREGRINE FALCON, THE FASTEST PREDATOR ON EARTH

SHE LAUNCHED HERSELF INTO THE AIR AND WITH FIVE POWERFUL WING BEATS ACHIEVED ENOUGH MOMENTUM TO STALL BRIEFLY, ERECT EACH FEATHER AND SHAKE OFF EVERY DROP OF RAIN.

It was her third hunt that day and with the sun low in the sky she made it with even more urgency. For three days, perhaps more, the weather and her inexperience had denied her the success of a kill. As a result, she was hungry, anxious and perhaps a little too eager.

Leaving the shelter of some rowan trees, she flew low across the peat bogs, hugging the contours of the land and following a small burn to the sea. Her passage was swift and silent, her presence, so far, unannounced. She was still perfecting her speed and agility, and now hunger lured her to the coast and the seabird colonies. There, she knew she had a better chance of taking a straggler in the flocks of waders gathering to roost.

At 70 kilometres an hour she came over a cliff edge. The land dropped 100 metres to the sea. A strong gust of wind brought the sound of crashing waves and the chatter of seabirds. It was, in human terms, like an armed robber walking out onto a busy street. Within a second a

Her eyes told me all about freedom.

thousand eyes had seen her and a hundred calls announced her. The whole colony was instantly on full alert. Birds dived for shelter and parents cowered over their remaining young. A gang of black-backed gulls tried to give chase, but they were no match for her aerial ability. She left them fussing far behind, soared high into the air and on to the estuary. The hunt had not yet begun.

North-west Scotland: a place of breathtaking beauty and home to an equally awe-inspiring creature – the peregrine falcon.

Aware of the fading light she picked up speed and turned south. Although not even a year old she was a highly effective aerial hunter. She had such powerful eyesight she could pinpoint her victims from more than a kilometre away. Short, sharp wings carried her streamlined, crow-sized body, wings so powerful they could hold her on course to impact a target at up to 200 kilometres an hour. At such incredible speeds she could expertly knock her prey out of the sky or grab it directly in mid-air.

She was a peregrine falcon, the fastest predator on earth.

High above the estuary and out of sight, she began to reconnoitre. From more than a kilometre away, she marked a small flock of waders on the shore. With the slightest alteration of her wings she banked and stooped, dropping like a stone. Bird and shadow flew in unison, low and fast across the ground. Like two projectiles they ripped across the landscape until, passing into shade, she was single once again. She was fast and focused and quickly closing in. The small flock of godwits were roosting, standing motionless with heads turned back over shoulders and beaks tucked under wings, some lightly sleeping. Nothing stirred except the occasional rocking of one of the guard birds.

The distant alarm call of a single curlew pierced the air. Almost simultaneously the godwits lifted their heads in search of danger. They looked and they listened, but no danger came.

For a moment the peace returned. But that was no false alarm. Suddenly, the whole estuary erupted in noise and motion. The godwits were airborne in an instant, and the falcon had one marked and was quickly closing in. As the falcon passed, other godwits threw themselves headfirst into the water in blind terror. The falcon locked onto her target and her focus was unfaltering. The target godwit rose and banked left, then right, then left again, the falcon effortlessly echoing the small bird's every move. In panic the godwit rose and fell, banked hard right, left and right, again and again trying desperately to out-fly her pursuer. In an instant they dropped landwards together, the godwit throwing itself towards the ground, racing, zigzagging for cover beyond a fence.

The falcon was doing over 100 kilometres an hour when she hit the wire. The bone snapped cleanly in two and, in a puff of feathers, her body was catapulted to the ground. For a moment all went blank. The

Cruising at 70 kph, she came over a cliff edge and the land dropped 100 metres away to the sea.

Adult peregrines like this one, with their beautiful slate–blue back, look more striking than juveniles like Alba who still had her immature brown plumage.

godwit rose into the air and made a wide arc to rejoin the circling flock. In unison they spiralled landwards and alighted on the sand, shuffled feathers, preened and chattered, sensing the danger was past.

The falcon felt more confusion than pain, until her senses warned her she was now in danger. She tried to launch herself into the air. Nothing happened. She tried again. On the ground and unable to fly, she was deluged with fear and panic. She again tried to fly, but it was useless, her wing was hanging limp and immobile. She preened its bloodied feathers till the pain made her stop. Gripping her feet and talons tight into the earth she looked about, staring and gasping for breath.

Two days later the falcon was discovered under a hedge by a sheepdog belonging to crofter Callum McRae, who recognised the bird as a "seabhag" – a peregrine – and phoned the "cruelty man", the Highland Region SSPCA inspector.

I THOUGHT I SHOULD KNOCK BEFORE ENTERING, SUCH WAS THE RESPECT SHE DESERVED. WITH A STOOL IN ONE HAND, MY PENCILS IN THE OTHER AND A SKETCHBOOK UNDER MY ARM, MY ENTRY WAS CLUMSY.

As I closed the door I was instantly conscious of the penetrating stare that had anticipated my arrival even before I reached the door. Its intensity was palpable. Like some awkward schoolboy I self-consciously arranged my stool below her, dropping a pencil. For the first time I looked up, but our eyes did not meet and her stare was now fixed on the pencil. Apologetically, I slowly crouched down to retrieve it. Her stare, still fixed on the pencil, followed my movement and continued slowly upwards until she was looking me straight in the eyes.

I felt obliged to say something complimentary. "Good evening, bonny lass," I whispered.

She kept staring. Anxious to get started, I sat down, gently turned the leaves of my sketchbook to a fresh sheet of paper and placed my hand on that lovely clean sheet, pencil poised. This was a rare opportunity indeed.

I looked up and our eyes met once again, her stare hadn't wavered. I wanted to start drawing straight away, but everything stayed motionless – our eye contact, our bodies and my pencils. She would do nothing but stare at me and contemplate. And I could do nothing except stare and admire.

I studied her subtle lines, patterns and colours. She was all I had expected – beautiful without doubt, but beneath that beauty, cold and calculating. She was small in size, but incredibly threatening. She was powerful and she was proud, and her eyes told me all about freedom. She was, after all, a peregrine falcon.

There was no doubt she was all of these things, but now she was also a cripple and a captive.

We'd had no prior notice of her arrival. One of the Highland inspectors simply turned up at Middlebank with a bird in a box, which I routinely took into the reception room and opened. I was stunned. A peregrine falcon is one of the rarest birds in Britain, and although I had seen and handled them before, I had never had the opportunity to look after one.

I felt a rush of excitement and a sense of honour that we had been given the responsibility for one of these awe-inspiring creatures. Whatever state they are in, they always have this air of menace, and she was giving me the peregrine's proud, self-righteous, "don't mess with me" sort of look. She was in a sorry state, with ruffled feathers and broken wing, bloodied, bruised and swollen. We could tell from her condition, and from the weather, that she had not eaten for days. Bad weather explained her over-eagerness to catch prey. In rain or fog a bird of prey will just sit and wait until the weather clears before hunting again. Youthful inexperience had also increased her chances of making mistakes in flight.

From her plumage we could tell she was young. Adult peregrine falcons are striking, with a beautiful slate-grey back. The males have a pinkish breast, distinctive spots down the front and a black moustache. Juveniles, like this one, are brown and their plumage is not as striking or distinct as the adult.

Before feeding her, it was important to find out the extent of her injuries. I donned thick gloves and held her powerful talons while the centre manager, Sandra Hogben, bathed her wounds. As the blood soaked from the feathers and the damage was revealed she remained motionless and her stare stayed fixed on our eyes. Birds of prey typically wait for the chance not, like other birds, to escape, but to fight back. She panted lightly in distress.

As we gently manipulated her wing we could hear the broken ends of bone grating together. She drew her head

A peregrine falcon can reach speeds of up to 200 kilometres an hour during a "stoop" – the mid-air dive during which it attempts to knock its prey out of the sky.

back and hissed, tightening her grip on my gloves. It was some handshake – about the full strength of a small human hand grip. We could feel that the break was at least clean, but the true extent of the damage, and her subsequent chances, could only be confirmed by x-rays at the local veterinary surgery.

It took about half an hour to clean her up and give her an injection of antibiotics, then I took her into a holding cage, placing a wooden block on the cage floor for her to perch on so she felt more secure. When "raptors" (the fancy word for birds of prey) are not engaging in aerial warfare or tending their young, they while away the hours watching the world (or, in Scotland, the rain) go by while digesting their victims. This activity obviously involves the frequent and copious redecoration of the immediate area from the rear, and to avoid the rather unsavoury soiling of their tails in unnatural captive surroundings, a raised wooden block is recommended. This simply takes the place of a branch or a rocky outcrop in the wild and keeps their delicate feathers out of harm's way.

Of equal concern are their feet. If kept on flat surfaces for too long a nasty condition called "bumblefoot" can develop, which is incurable and can permanently damage or handicap the foot. As she took happily to the wooden block my mind turned to an issue that was almost certainly nagging at hers – food.

I entered the holding room with my offering and placed it gently in front of our new patient. She stared at it. Then she stared at me, with an expression that was clearly willing me out of the room. "Here, bonny lass," I said, "have three dead chickens, headless, legless and all of them freshly skinned . . . yuk." I shut the cage door and left her to feed. I had little doubt that she would – most birds of prey are not shy when it comes to free meat.

I left her undisturbed overnight before donning gloves the following morning and taking her in a secure box to the local vet's for her x-rays. Today I wanted to hang around to see the x-rays immediately and also, as usual, to protect Joe Ryan, our long-suffering vet, from the latest nasty piece of work.

Ryan and Calder were one of the nearest veterinary practices to the centre and, like most in Britain, they didn't have much formal training in wildlife rehab, especially avian wildlife. It was very much a learning curve, but they were very obliging and helpful. They did admit it was very often trial and error, and a matter of doing their best with the challenges we brought in. And, if that wasn't enough, they sometimes got expert help or specialist treatment – as with the swan they sent for an endoscopy in Glasgow.

They were a married couple in their late thirties. Joe was quite a big

She had a mesmerising stare, as if the only way she had left of exerting her power was by willing me to leave the room.

Opposite: It was some handshake, about the strength of a small human grip. Her talons were needle sharp and highly efficient at ripping flesh.

burly guy, with milk bottle specs and dark hair, very easy-going and relaxed with a great sense of humour, and he seemed to enjoy seeing what surprise I had for him. I think we were a bit of light relief in his daily practice.

"Well, what have you got to threaten my manhood this time? That ruddy seal I injected last week got me a beauty, right where it hurts. Nearly settled negotiations with Aileen and I on the potential for our second child. Did you see it?"

"Not sure I want to," I said.

"No, the seal, you Wally. Right, now what's it going to do to me . . . and what weapons does it possess?"

I placed the box gently on the table, and motioned for him to let me open it.

"It's more the grip of this one than the bite," I grinned, enjoying the wind-up. "Don't worry, you won't lose anything precious, and I'll hold on tight."

"Aye, I've heard you say that before." Joe was looking very smug as he reached into a cupboard. "I now have the perfect protection," and he turned round holding something large and leather that resembled half a pair of waders.

"Sent away for it last week. Isn't it brilliant?" He looked and sounded delighted as he started putting it on or rather climbing into it. "You know those police dog demonstrations, the ones where the pretend robber runs across the car park and they set the dogs on him? Well . . . ."

I roared with laughter.

"Only kidding," he said. "I was given it. God knows what it's for, but you never know." He put it back in the cupboard. I gloved up and opened the box. Gently grasping the falcon and holding her wings tight to her body I placed her on the table, making certain to maintain a firm grip.

"Well, well . . . where did you get that from?" Joe was suitably impressed.

"Isn't she the business?" I said, as pleased as punch. "Just in from the Outer Hebrides. She's come a long way and unfortunately her journey was assisted. She must have flown into something." Joe was shaking his head in sympathy. "The right humerus is snapped," I said, "but it seems pretty clean . . . see what you think." As I held tightly, Joe gently manipulated the broken wing and assessed the extent of her injury.

"It could quite easily be pinned," he said, "let's take some x-rays and have a better look." After what proved to be a bit of a performance, with me getting more radiation than the bird, Joe came back with the developed x-rays.

Opposite: Her powerful eyesight could pinpoint her victims from over a kilometre away.

"Your hands came out a treat, looks like there are still five fingers on each. Look . . . ."

He held the x-ray to the light box. "Okay, joking aside, as we thought it's a very clean break and we can place a pin from here to here – that should hold it and be pretty straightforward. But look at this in her right thigh."

Joe pointed at a solid mass which showed up as a white spot on the x-ray.

"I don't believe it," I looked at him in disbelief. "That looks like lead shot."

"Sure does."

"Christ, some bastard's taken a shot at her . . . . What the hell?"

"Looks like it, doesn't it? Doesn't appear to be causing her too much trouble thank heavens, but we'll remove it during the pinning just to make sure."

"She's not even a year old. What's wrong with folk, Joe?"

"Ha . . . people. Try attending some of my midnight call-outs," he said. "Most animals have more of a clue. Still, that's life." We were agreed on that point.

"Right," he said, turning to his surgery appointments book, "how about Friday? We'll book her in after lunch and Aileen and I will give it a go. Has it got a name?"

"Aye, she certainly has. It's Alba."

"Albu what? . . . as in Albuquerque?"

"No, ya ninny . . . Alba, it's Gaelic for Scotland."

"Och aye, silly me, so it is. Fine name – why Alba?"

"I wanted something that suggested a thing of wild beauty and the fight for freedom."

"God, you artists . . ." he said, shaking his head and scribbling in the book. "She's down for after lunch . . . . I suppose you have half the falconers in Scotland banging on your door by now?"

"No, not yet, but no doubt we will when the word gets out," I replied.

He thought of something. "Now listen," said Joe, "Peregrines, they're a schedule one protected species, aren't they?"

"Aye, they most certainly are, there's only about a thousand in the country." There were even fewer in the 1960s, and it was the usual story – they were hammered badly by pesticides. But now the falcon population was recovering and they had full protection. This was great but it brought with it the added attention of a raft of experts.

"Will you have to pass her on?"

"Almost certainly," I replied. "If the pinning works she'll be in captivity for some time, right?"

Opposite: She could do nothing but stare at me and contemplate . . . I could do nothing but stare and admire.

Alba, born to rule the turbulent skies of the Highlands, was destined to spend the rest of her life in captivity.

"That's for sure . . . it'll take a long time to heal."

"Beyond our legal holding period then?"

"Perhaps worse . . . perhaps forever," said Joe raising his eyebrows. All birds of prey had to be registered with the Department of the Environment after six weeks, and to become a licensed raptor keeper, or LRK, you had to have proper facilities and expertise. We probably could have got a licence at Middlebank, but, apart from baby owls in spring, we rarely kept raptors for long enough to need one.

Alba was our first peregrine and, with all the attention her rarity attracted amongst licensed raptor keepers, her future was to be decided by more executive powers than mine. The network of LRKs and the Ministry of the Environment would take her off our hands, and I was actually quite relieved (although annoyed at the same time by the implication that we didn't have the expertise to look after her). We were especially busy, and giving the peregrine to a licensed facility was like putting her into intensive care and would only be good for the bird.

I spent a great deal of the week or so we had remaining before her operation finding excuses to pass her cage and admire her, and she spent most of it eating headless, day-old chickens. On Friday I returned her to the veterinary surgery and sat uneasily for the rest of the day in the office wondering how she was getting on. At last the phone rang, and it was Joe.

"Success?" I asked eagerly.

"Yep, pretty straightforward," he said. "The pin worked well, but I think it might even be best left in there for good. I doubt she'll ever see true freedom again, though. She'll never be a hundred percent, but I think we knew that, didn't we?"

"Aye, well, she's alive. And what about the lead shot?"

"It was a gunshot pellet, that's for sure. I'll show you it later when you pick her up. Do you want it as a memento?"

"No, but I know what I'd like to do with it," I said.

"Absolutely," he replied.

So now, as I sat on my stool trying to sketch her on her last night with us, I could do little but stare into her eyes, those eyes that still tried to tell me all about freedom. I managed a few lines but that was all. I was too busy listening.

The following day I parted company with Alba and she left to spend life with a raptor keeper licensed in southern Scotland. Although she would never see true freedom again it was decided that she could be trained as a falconer's bird. Using the lure of food as a reward she would learn quickly not to fly far from the fist, not that she could even do that well now.

Perhaps at some summer country fair she sits regally perched on a falconer's gloved fist, her head shrouded in a decorative hood to keep her from startling or becoming too lively. Leather jesses attach one leg to the glove. A bell attached to her tail jingles with every footstep. Above the noise of the bell she can hear other noises, which she is, by now, used to – voices, laughter, dogs barking. She is alert and hungry and knows a reward is imminent. As her hood is removed she loses balance slightly and flaps her wings – one of which is not quite straight. She folds them again then grasps the perch that she has been placed on and is rewarded with a yellow day-old chicken. Before ripping it apart she looks out at her spectators.

She stares and she contemplates. And they stare back and admire. Was she not, after all, a peregrine falcon . . . the fastest predator on earth?

Yes . . . and no. She was Alba, captive falcon, and if you knew to look a little closer you might just be able to see that her eyes could no longer tell you all about freedom.

Neist Point, Duirinish, Isle of Skye off the north-west coast of Scotland, one of the few remaining habitats of the fastest predator on earth.

HUEY, DEWEY & LOUIE

TAWNY OWLETS THREE, CRAIGALISTAIR THUGS NIL

"ALL WE NEED NOW IS A SPANISH DANCER," I THOUGHT AS I PLACED THREE ANGRY OWL CHICKS IN THE RECEPTION ROOM. THEY SOUNDED LIKE CASTANETS: "SNAP, SNAP . . . SNAP, SNAP . . . SNAP, SNAP, SNAP . . ." SSPCA CHIEF INSPECTOR ANDY INNES HAD JUST BROUGHT THEM IN, AND THE OWLETS, TRUE TO FORM, WERE SNAPPING THEIR BEAKS AS THEIR WAY OF ISSUING A WARNING.

"So, Andy, isn't this the second batch of owl chicks from your area this week?" He nodded rather grimly. "What's going on?" He'd brought in six owl chicks so far and it was still only the beginning of spring.

"Well, the first lot was found by a dog and this batch I had been keeping an eye on," said Andy. "I knew about the nest site, it's been used by a pair of tawnies for years and always causes problems. Every damn year it's the same."

"Why?" I asked, "or can I guess?"

"They're hardly wise old owls. They set up home across the road from the Craigalistair estate, and the thugs finally got their bloody hands on them, as usual."

Owl chicks were extremely vulnerable between leaving the nest and learning to fly. It was at that stage that they turned up at Middlebank.

Every spring we were delivered what looked like bundles of grey cotton wool by concerned members of the public.

Opposite: "Brancher" owl chicks sometimes fall from their perches to the woodland floor, where they instantly attract the attention of foxes, cats and dogs, and, of course, human beings.

I felt a sickening feeling. I wasn't going to like what I'd hear. Owl chicks were extremely vulnerable between leaving the nest and learning to fly. It was the main reason we got them at Middlebank.

"These three hadn't even left the nest. The kids raided it and . . . well, I can't believe it really. Then again, perhaps I can . . ." Andy said, with a pained expression.

"Tell me about it. What were they doing to them this time?"

I didn't feel good about the look of revulsion on Andy's face. "Playing football with them!" he said. It was one of those "Can you believe it?" statements. Even this hardened inspector, who had seen the worst humans could do to animals, was shocked.

"You're joking?" I felt myself going rigid with rage. "No wonder they're bloody angry. Did you get the little bastards?"

"I wasn't there. It was an elderly couple that saw them. The boys were about to take a penalty with one of the owls into the couple's driveway, which they were using as a goal. Thankfully the kids ran off when they were confronted by the couple."

Above and below: A few days after they hatch, owl chicks start to resemble small, white earmuffs.

"Oh, that's a blessing," I said sarcastically, "I wouldn't have put it past them to use the old folks as goal posts." For me it was like there were two different and irreconcilable worlds, my world of wildlife rescue and the countryside, and the bleak wasteland of the housing estates where, it seemed, some people had lost all feeling for nature. But at least the old folks still had a heart. "How do you put up with it Andy? I would get done for murder if I did your job."

"Well it certainly takes a lot of patience and self-control."

"Too right! Anyway, thanks for bringing the owl chicks in, I'm sure they'll survive. Any particular names you want to christen them? Cartoon characters are the theme just now."

We settled on Huey, Dewey and Louie, and I signed them into the arrivals book. At Middlebank we looked after many tawny owls. Every spring cages would fill with what looked like bundles of grey cotton wool, only their huge black eyes, hooked beak and sharp talons giving them away as owls and not cuddly toys. They usually arrived singly, sometimes up to three at a time from the same nest. Owls commonly hatch two to four eggs and raise that number of chicks to young adulthood, although there is a mortality rate. Its fluctuations depend on weather, season, food availability and mishap.

Within a few days young owls are already taking on the appearance of small, white earmuffs and within two to three weeks they are already 15–20 centimetres tall. When they are too big for the nest they simply shift onto a nearby branch, where they perch waiting for the conscientious parent, usually the male, to bring food at regular intervals.

"Branchers", as the owlets are called, are not just sitting around; they are busy absorbing from the adults the business of hunting. As gorgeously endearing as owls look, with their massive dark, beautiful eyes and cute proportions, their role in the countryside is the same as that of the shark in the ocean: they are predators, ruthless and efficient, preying on the weak and helpless, a role as essential to the balance of nature as that of any other creature.

Sometimes, after an early unsuccessful attempt at flight or due to high winds, brancher owl chicks fall to the woodland floor, where they are immediately vulnerable to the attentions of foxes and other creatures, especially humans. If left undisturbed the parents will continue feeding the owlets on the ground. But because they're such fluffy and enchanting little things, it's no wonder people pick them up and "rescue" them, often bringing them to us at Middlebank.

Very occasionally, provided we were quick, we could return the owl chicks to where they were found. Sometimes, we could even relocate chicks to other nests and with other parents. But, usually, by the time we received them the bewildered creatures had been round all the kids in the neighbourhood before eventually being found by Mum in the dolls' pram, by Dad in his golf bag or by the family pet in its bed.

I must admit to frequently being guilty of such well-intentioned but misguided rescue efforts myself as a child. The art of hand rearing owl chicks is actually very easy. In fact, compared to other young animals, especially seals, it is positively delightful. Owls and other birds of prey have a voracious appetite. It doesn't matter to chicks who's feeding them, they just grab what's on offer and down the hatch it goes. It usually takes only a minute, perhaps a few hours or, less often, days before the clever little soul realises he or she is onto a good thing.

Young owls generally survived with us into adulthood, provided they were not too thin, too wet and chilled, or injured by jaws or human hands.

Although enraged by their treatment at the hands of spotty-faced

Tawny owlets will show interest in eating anything that moves or makes a noise and consequently they enjoy an extensive and somewhat gruesome menu. We fed them day-old dead chickens.

delinquents, Huey, Dewey and Louie were uninjured and more than willing to eat. We became the fast food suppliers. The source was, I'm afraid to say, day-old chickens. We took the place of parent owl, tearing morsels off the chickens and presenting them to the eagerly watching owl chicks. After a very short time we just put the whole chickens into the cage and the owlets did the rest. It was quite comical to watch. Their eyes would open wide as if half in fear and half in delight and they would snap their beaks in threat between mouthfuls, until their eyes began to close in satisfaction and the snapping became less energetic, finally fading away completely as their stomachs got fuller and fuller.

With such five-star treatment it was little wonder the triplets grew quickly and spent most of their time sleeping. You might expect owls, with their image as wise old keepers of the forest, to sleep with some decorum, but owlets would spread-eagle themselves on the cage floor with their legs in the air as if the world was their duvet, and snooze till the next mealtime.

For the purposes of identification and record keeping we ringed the legs of the owls, but we could often tell them apart by the differences in their appearance, character and colouring. Huey was always a middle-sized bird, but made up for that by being the loudest and most snappy. Louie was noticeably the bravest, being the largest and most robust, and was always trying to get out of the cage. Dewey, who I presumed was the last out of the egg, was smaller than the other siblings and the sleepiest.

The plumage of all tawny owls is exquisite, varying from shades of orange-brown through dark brown to grey. I am particularly fond of owls for another reason too: their smell. Adults have a wonderful, woody smell which is hard to define. It's not the rotting leaf smell of leaf mould. I can only call it a woodland scent, which I recognise as the smell of a deciduous wood in Britain. Other birds don't really have

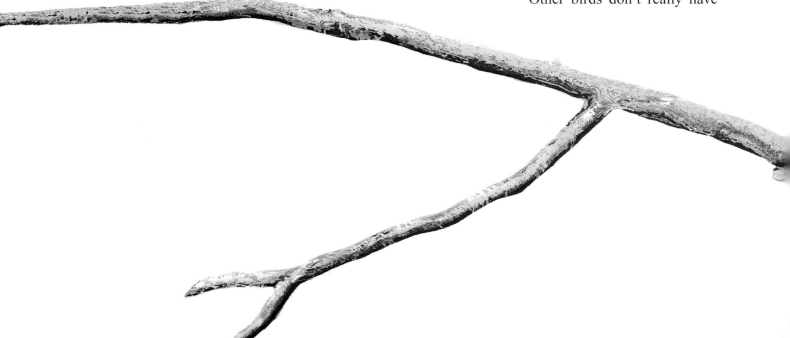

smells that I remember in particular except seabirds, whose distinctive odour is more from their excrement than their plumage.

Huey, Dewey and Louie were delightfully easy-going residents at Middlebank and they grew furiously. Release, however, was a long way off. Until their feathers had emerged through the downy cotton wool and their wings could support their weight in flight, this would be their home.

They looked hilarious as their feathers started to come through around the edges of their facial disc. Then gradually their body, flight and tail feathers appeared, unfurling from shafts and emerging from the down like unfolding petals. Only by handling wild birds can you fully appreciate the incredible design, complexity and beauty of feathers.

Tawny owls have adapted to an extraordinary degree to their role as forest predator. Their wing feathers have very fine, broken edges and a velvety pile over the surface which deadens the noise of their wing beats in flight. When you stand in an aviary and they're flying around your head the silence is ominous. Their prey must have little or no warning of attack, and so successful are the owls that I wouldn't fancy my chances as a mouse scurrying around the forest floor.

It always amuses me that the United States spends millions of dollars on developing a Stealth bomber when nature, over about the same number of years, has perfected a design for owls far simpler and with far less fuss. Despite our seemingly incredible human creations, nature has many ways of making us look amateurish.

AT ABOUT FIVE OR SIX WEEKS THE OWLETS WERE BIG AND STRONG ENOUGH TO BE PUT OUTSIDE IN OUR LARGE PURPOSE-BUILT AVIARIES. UNTIL THEY DEVELOPED WINGS THIS WAS A BIT OF A NON-EVENT FOR THEM, BUT FOR US IT WAS GREAT NEWS.

With a creche of up to six owlets per aviary, they were a breeze to look after. Aside from a daily feed and a twice-daily check they could be left to sleep and grow, and we turned our attentions to force feeding seal pups.

If I ever felt under stress and was dizzy with all the many, varied and unpredictable activities that came our way at a rehab centre, there was no better escape, no better haven to retreat to with a cup of coffee, than the owl aviary. There, the scene and the mood resembled some sort of Roman bathhouse or Buddhist meditation session. Relaxation and digestion were the key activities. Perhaps one or two eyes half opened to check on your presence, but the owls were not bothered at all if you sat quietly in the aviary to watch, admire or, at the end of a working day, join in and snooze. Whenever my colleagues went to look for me, if I wasn't wrestling seals or taking photographs they would usually find me in blissful peace and self-administered therapy with the owls.

Huey, Dewey and Louie had arrived in April and stayed until nearly November. By then we had anything from 12 to 20 young owls to release. The triplets looked very handsome in their near-adult plumage and now had an entirely different and much more distinguished upright sleeping pose. Tawny owls are nocturnal, of course, and spend the daylight hours roosting and half dozing.

Being birds of prey they cannot afford to do this conspicuously because they could then be subject to the irate, repetitive protestations of smaller birds intent on letting the entire neighbourhood know of the owl's presence.

I always thought their comings and goings were a bit like the Prime Minister slipping in and out of No. 10 Downing Street during a demonstration, but instead of an anonymous pinstripe suit, newspaper and darkened limousine, owls use their brown camouflage plumage and shape to avoid detection. With inimitable guile they stretch themselves lengthwise, wings tight against their sides so they have no obvious angles, close their eyes (but not always shut) and perch cleverly next to a tree trunk

An inquisitive nature is important to a young predator. Anything that comes within range of a baby owl (that is not sleeping) will come under close scrutiny.

Opposite: Tawnies have a particular, and for me evocative, smell of the woods they inhabit.

Previous page: In the owl aviary the scene and mood resembled my idea of a Roman bathhouse or Buddhist meditation session. Relaxation and digestion were the key activities and sometimes, after my lunch, I'd hide myself away and join them in a snooze.

When presented with food their eyes would open wide as if half in fear and half in delight.

Opposite: Owls are the forest's detectives, specialists at hiding where they can quietly watch you unable to watch them.

for camouflage. There, like small lifeless Egyptian statuettes, confident and inscrutably wise, they watch others who are unable to watch them, until night falls and the potential protesters all go off to roost.

Then the owl awakes. Deliberately one large and ominous dark eye opens, followed by the other, and those great, beautiful, luminous discs seem to pool and store the moon's light for the coming night of espionage before the owl silently sets off to prey on the weak and unsuspecting.

With the Middlebank owls, raised as they were on a perpetual free lunch, we could not just open the aviary door and wish them luck because they had not yet had any practice at hunting. In the wild, through instinct and the teachings of their wise old parent, young owls learn to hunt food quickly, and even if they fail to begin with there is always a parent on hand with back-up supplies.

Obviously an owl parent is far more adept at teaching and attending to their offspring than humans and, more importantly, she has the time. Middlebank in early summer was like the lost and found department of a huge toy shop in the week before Christmas. We were rushed off our feet bribing fledglings, waifs and strays to eat. And the problem was that, unlike the human lost and found department, Mum never turned up, so we were stuck with the lot of them.

Our method of returning young owls to the wild was called "hacking back", a common procedure when releasing captive wildlife back where they belong. The concept is simple in theory, if not always in practice. The idea is to give the creature a gradual reintroduction over a period of weeks. While still providing food at the same time every day, you allow them access in and out of the aviary.

Occasionally some over-eager youngster would dash out of the aviary with its equivalent of the human "Yee-haa", and all you could see was its bottom, a mere blur in the wild blue yonder. But fortunately sudden escape attempts were quite rare.

We tried to release owls back where they had been found, but that was not often possible. We had to have someone living close by who was available and willing to take care of this transition.

The Huey, Dewey and Louie release was textbook. We relocated all three to a small mobile aviary in a private woodland a stone's throw from a friend's house. Alan Hilton lived just across the Firth of Forth and was responsible at the time for ringing our birds before release. (To "ring" a bird means to put plastic or metal bands inscribed with an identifying series of numbers or letters around its leg.)

Huey, Dewey and Louie arrived at Alan's in their own roosting box from Middlebank, the one they were accustomed to sleeping in. Alan would

Perhaps one or two eyes would half open to check on your presence, but that was all.

provide food at the same time every day, usually around dusk when owls begin to rise and shine. For the first week their cage was kept shut, until they were used to the sights and sounds of this new environment. Then the aviary roof was opened and it was up to them if they came home for tea.

For about a week all three of them were there when Alan came to feed them. Then Louie, always the bravest, did not show for two nights. This was not necessarily cause for concern. On the contrary, it probably meant he was beginning to catch food for himself – worms or beetles to begin with. Any morsel of nutrition moving on the ground at night is detected by the owl's highly acute sense of hearing.

In the days, weeks and months to come Louie would graduate to larger prey like mice and voles, and, if he were really clever, the occasional avian protester on its way home to roost.

To encourage the birds further towards independence, the amount of food Alan left out was gradually decreased. After about a month, no more food or pocket money was supplied and the adolescents were forced to go out and earn their own living. Luckily, most birds, and especially owls, are well brought-up adolescents and eager to leave home. Huey, Dewey and Louie all finally disappeared.

Sadly, that autumn brave Louie was found dead on a busy road nearby after an argument with a car, one of the most common causes of death for owls. Disappointing as that was, we were encouraged because he was in excellent condition. At least we knew our owl-rearing programme worked and that his sister and brother were most probably out there somewhere, hiding up a tree watching you unable to watch them, catching mice, taking their rightful place in the world and generally having a hoot.

Adult tawnies' exquisite plumage carries all the shades and tones and subtleties of colour from dull grey to bright orange.

The shot I wanted would make a wonderful composition — the upright sweep of the worn wooden spade handle continued by the upward sweep of the sleeping owl. It was albit mean, but I took all the perches out of the aviary and dug the spade into the floor. When I got back, there was Louie, perched asleep on the handle. I had only one chance because as soon as the flash went off the owl would wake and fly away. I knew in my heart when I pressed the shutter I had a great picture.

Then it occurred to me that I had two more owls and spades . . . "If you get that it'll be an absolute cracker," I thought. Serendipity is the only word for it. There they were, three owls dozing like a row of statues. "Ya beauty," I whispered as the shutter clicked. I entitled this picture "Tawnies on a Teabreak".

SLIPPER

A GREY SQUIRREL GOES SHOPPING

"OCH . . . THAT'LL BE THE PHONE. BLOODY THING ALWAYS RINGS WHEN I'M OOT IN THE YARD . . . I'M GETTING TOO AULD FAE THIS." HARRY NICHOLSON, THE SSPCA CHIEF INSPECTOR FOR DUNDEE, WAS NEARING RETIREMENT AND HOBBLED WITH A MARKED LIMP. "I'LL SEE YOU SOON NOO DARROCH, FEED A SEAL ON ME, EH," HE SHOUTED OVER HIS SHOULDER WITH A WAVE. I COULD HEAR HIM CHUCKLING TO HIMSELF AS HE HEADED BACK INTO THE OFFICE.

I'd travelled the 80 kilometres from Middlebank to pick up some supplies from the Dundee office. For once I was looking forward to having nothing in the back of the van with fish-breath or loose bowels, or that made excruciating noises. The fresh air and the silence would be golden, I thought happily. I should have known better. It was, after all, only mid-morning.

As I sparked the van into life, I watched through the window as Harry's

The grey squirrel, both loved and hated.

Squirrels are expert climbers and very fast and agile, particularly when cornered.

lips moved and he nodded in reply to whoever he was talking with on the phone. I was trying to catch his eye once again to wave, when he gesticulated anxiously for me to wait a minute and hobbled out. I wound down the window. "Are you in a rush?" he asked. It was a leading question.

"Not really, why?"

"Well, believe it or not, there's a squirrel apparently running around a shoe shop in the town centre."

"There never is!" I chuckled.

Harry's world-weary look and shake of the head said it all. "Okay, no problem Harry . . . I'm the fit young lad and the wildlife lover, I'll attend to it, shall I?"

"Och, will you?" he cheered up. "That's ma boy. We're awfie busy."

"Try stopping me," I said. I was, in fact, delighted with the prospect.

Half way there I realised that in my eagerness I had forgotten the first golden rule of wildlife rescue – go prepared. I had no gloves and, what's more, no box. What I needed was a cat box, I thought, but the next best thing . . . a shoe box, of course . . . brilliant. But what was a squirrel doing in a shoe shop, and how would I catch it?

If this were Edinburgh, where there were squirrels living in parks in the centre of town, it wouldn't have been such a surprise, but I knew that there weren't that many squirrels in Dundee, let alone the town centre.

Each year we received many calls about injured squirrels, even though many people considered them a pest. I'd fed tame squirrels in parks and I'd handled red squirrels. But I had never handled an adult grey squirrel before. I felt certain it would be a grey squirrel because they are the only one of the two species in Britain which inhabits town centres. And if greys were anything like red squirrels it was going to be a bit like catching a bar of soap with your teeth under water. Somehow I knew this would be fun.

After parking the van I hurried down Murraygate, the busy main street, dodging shoppers, bags and prams, and looking up at shop frontages for the shoe shop sign. I realised I must have looked like a member of the armed offenders squad because I could see I was getting odd glances and could hear whispered comments as I passed. My militaristic appearance was partly due to my official uniform, similar to a probationary inspector's, and partly because of my own modifications to it.

The SSPCA was founded in Victorian times to prevent cruelty to animals, particularly to horses used for transport, and its inspectors were empowered to search and execute warrants, in conjunction with the police. The uniform today still resembles the police uniform, with dark navy jacket, epaulettes and silver pips indicating ranks from inspector to chief inspector, and even a cap with chin strap.

I had felt a bit ridiculous walking around looking like a police inspector, so I had modified my uniform to suit my particular job. At Middlebank we didn't fit into the overall scheme of things anyway, in terms of SSPCA ranking. I wore my uniform to and from work, but as soon as I arrived in the morning I put on overalls because of the strong likelihood of being sprayed and covered in excrement of various shapes, consistencies and sizes. If you were at all squeamish, you wouldn't go anywhere near wildlife rehabilitation.

My own modifications to the official uniform included the addition of a black photographer's flak jacket, the type with lots of useful pockets, and I had put an official SSPCA badge on the chest pocket. I had also found myself some black, commando-type trousers with pockets on the legs and sides, and with regulation Doc Marten boots I seriously resembled a paratrooper from one of those Los Angeles SWAT teams.

Before too many bystanders had stopped to watch, I spotted the shoe shop and ducked inside. What I saw stopped me in my tracks – it was a scene of devastation. There were no customers. Shoe boxes and shoes of all sizes from infant to adult were jumbled and piled around the walls. In the middle of the mess, down on her knees amongst a pile of training shoes, a young shop assistant was sobbing as she replaced shoes in boxes.

"Oh dear," I said in sympathy. It was hilarious, but this was no time to let my professional guard slip.

"I thought it was a rat," she cried, "a big bloody rat," and she burst into tears again.

At that, a young man came barrelling out of the office at the back of the shop nursing his finger.

"Ah . . . you'll be Rentokil, or is it the cruelty society . . . ? God, who did I phone?" He was almost equally distraught.

"Well, you got it right, I'm SSPCA. So where is it?"

"You're too late," he said, pressing a plaster around his finger, "it's buggered off. Marie stop crying, it was a squirrel, for crying out loud."

"It was nae . . . I tell ya, it was a bloody great rat. Basta' did the wall o' death roon the shop then shot oot the door wi' the customers . . . and one had new shoes on . . . and he has nae paid." She began to bawl again.

"Where did it go?" I asked, trying desperately to keep a straight face.

"I heard someone say it went three doors down into Pro-Performance."

"Okay, thanks," I said, turning towards the door. "What's Pro-Performance?"

"Another shoe shop," said the manager looking bewildered.

"What . . . it never is!" I said with a grin. "Right, thanks for calling us." And I shot out the door.

Overleaf: For his portrait session Slipper was handled with thick gloves. For his capture I was not so fortunate.

I felt nothing but sympathy for my wee shoe shopper and thought his crime that day was hardly so serious as to be punishable by death.

Opposite: At last, between a size six and a size nine sports shoe, I could see the object of all the hysteria.

I pushed through the crowds and continued looking at shop signs, but it was a sound that directed me. I heard a blood-curdling scream from a shop a short distance away. "That'll be it," I muttered to myself with a grin. As I hurtled into the shop, I was nearly knocked over by a middle-aged lady hurtling out.

"A flying rat," she cried. "My God, there's a flying rat in there," and she disappeared into the street and found safety in a gathering throng of onlookers.

I could understand why she, too, thought it was a flying rat. Squirrels move amazingly fast. They can jump nearly two metres along the ground, possibly further when alarmed, and move at nearly 30 kilometres an hour – an incredible speed for such a small creature. They move even faster and more easily when climbing, and when we had them at the centre there was no way to catch them in such a big space as an aviary. The only thing to do was to wait until they had gone into a nesting box, block off the entrance and open the back to capture them.

Inside this shoe shop I was confronted by a similar scene of devastation. Shoes littered the carpet, and this time the shop assistant was bracing herself against the storeroom door. She looked terrified.

"Oh, thank God you're here," she gasped, spotting the letters SSPCA. "I've trapped it in the storeroom."

"Okay," I said warily, "how big is it?"

"Oh, it's massive and all hairy with big bucked teeth. Is it a squirrel?"

"No, the storeroom," I said, "how big is it?"

"Och, the storeroom. It's pretty small." That was good news. If still at large in the shoe shop, the best I could have done was try to chase it out the front door or drive it into the back office.

"Okay," I said, "I'm going to go in and catch it, are you ready?"

"Brilliant," she said, moving aside while still clutching the door handle. "One . . . two . . . three . . . ," and with that she opened the door.

"I may be some time," I said as I brushed past her. Inside there was silence. My eyes adjusted to the darkened room and I stood scanning first the floor, then the desk, then a shelf of shoe boxes that went all the way to the ceiling. Between a size six and a size nine sports shoe, I spotted some grey fur and rapidly twitching whiskers. The squirrel's stare was unflinching. As I crouched to get a better look its whiskers twitched even faster. A grey squirrel, unlike the reports I'd been getting, is hardly massive. It's only the size of a small rabbit, and half of that is tail.

The poor creature was knackered by this stage, and obviously frightened. Wildlife will stand still, almost as if they believe you can't see

them if they don't move, and wait for an opportunity to make a dash for it.

"Now then . . . please, for your sake make this simple," I said as I made ready to pounce.

I approached very slowly, like a cat hunting, my hands steadily reaching out ahead of me, waiting for the right moment. In the blink of an eye the squirrel turned on its feet and leapt into the air. It sailed across the office and landed on a box marked "invoices".

"Okay, this time, wee man." Again I approached, and again it got ready to leap. But it was slightly cornered, and if it was going anywhere it would have to be over my head. Screeching in defiance it leapt once again, and with a lunge and a catch the envy of any wicket keeper, I grabbed hold of him. "How's zeee," I cried, then "aoww yaah," I shrieked, as two big incisors broke my skin. Squirrels have very sharp claws for climbing and long, sharp front incisors like rodents, shrews and mice.

Somehow, hardened by a job where I was constantly being bitten, I held on. Considering the squirrel was by now hanging off me like a bizarre piece of body piercing, I actually didn't have much choice. Unlike a bird of prey, which will bite and fix onto its victim, a squirrel will try and bite repeatedly. Luckily I was able to get control of the head, by holding the jaws and the base of the skull, and release my poor finger.

Grabbing a shoe box, I dumped out the contents and hastily replaced them with the squirrel, jamming the lid on to secure its capture so I could turn my attention to my wounds. To a round of applause I came out of the office, clutching my bleeding finger. The whole manoeuvre had taken about 10 minutes.

"Och, yer a hero," said the assistant, with a twinkle in her eye. She found a box of sticking plasters. "Here, let me." I didn't put up much of a struggle. After a few minutes of basking in adulation I made my excuses, grabbed the twitching shoe box and hurried back to the van.

I didn't have a clue where to release the squirrel in Dundee and, anyway, I felt inclined to line it up for my regulation mug shots. There wasn't anything wrong with the squirrel, and as I drove back down to Middlebank I pondered my dilemma. Grey squirrels are classified as a pest species and can be legally hunted by humans. But it is illegal for humans to import, keep or release grey squirrels from captivity without a licence from the Secretary of State for Scotland. I was fully aware of the law and the ridiculous fact that unless I killed my captive I was in the wrong. For me, killing was categorically out of the question.

If you were hard-line about pest species you'd destroy these animals, no matter in what circumstances you came across them. Yet I felt nothing but

When native (left) meets immigrant (right) conflicts occur – but I wasn't going to concern myself with the rights and wrongs of the territory dispute. In this case I felt there was only an individual to consider.

sympathy for my wee shoe shopper and felt his crime that day was hardly serious enough to be punishable by death. But the law was there for a reason – greys at times could be considered pests and did kill other wildlife when raiding nests for eggs or fledglings. They did a certain amount of damage to crops and gardens, and there was little doubt they were affecting the indigenous red squirrel population, so I felt a twinge of hypocrisy.

Wherever there has been a fight for habitat, the larger and more aggressive grey squirrels have pushed the reds out. The grey squirrel is not native to Scotland. Deliberately introduced, they arrived by boat in the 1890s from Canada and made claim to three sites in the central lowlands. They were a clever, capable lot and were delighted with their new surroundings, adapting very quickly. In fact, they flourished. Now, a hundred years on, indigenous reds are becoming scarce and it would seem the greys have just about taken over completely.

But given the fact that this grey squirrel had obviously come from an urban environment, where only his kind could thrive and where red squirrels and rare birds were not often found, I decided to release him somewhere similar.

Slipper, as he was now called, was given a day's respite in my own home, despite his pest status. This allowed me time to take some photographs and consider his fate. The following day I headed for the park in Dunfermline, where some of his grey relatives lived and no reds were known to reside. It was a fairly large area of old, established deciduous trees and well-manicured gardens. There was a chance that he would be turfed out by other grey squirrels, but it was better odds than he'd get elsewhere. Quietly and discreetly I took the shoe box into the park. As I set its contents free under a bush I sensed the twitching of other interested whiskers.

"Good luck," I whispered as he bounced away into the undergrowth. I sat a moment in the autumn twilight thinking. The land struggles of these small creatures mirrored our own conflicts in Scotland and the problems of colonisation all over the world. It was we humans who were responsible for bringing grey squirrels across the Atlantic, because they most definitely would never have swum across otherwise.

I wondered who was right and who was wrong, what we humans were doing about this 100-year struggle and if there would ever be a solution. I was certain of one thing, though. Wildlife or human, introduced or indigenous, whatever the conflicts and disagreements, there was always the individual to consider. I had no regrets about giving Slipper his freedom.

TRIPOLI

A SWAN LOVE STORY

1 FELT TROUBLED AND ILL AT EASE AS I APPROACHED THE LONGANNET POWER STATION. IT LOOKED LIKE THE GATES OF HELL. A CLOAK OF BLACK CLOUD HUNG ACROSS THE FIRTH, STAINED ORANGE BY THE LIGHT OF THE OIL REFINERY FLARES IN THE DISTANCE AT GRANGEMOUTH.

It was all so dark and threatening, so industrial and human-made, that for a minute I felt an edge of panic and thought about retreating. But this was the right place.

The Middlebank centre is on the south-west coast of the Firth of Forth. The Firth is scenic in part, like the tiny historic village of Limekilns where I lived and the Victorian Forth rail bridge, famous for its three spans of intricate red iron lacework. But other areas of the waterway, like this huge power station I was approaching, were highly industrialised and polluted. I drove the van up to the main gates and waited for the barriers to rise. The security guard in a booth nearby chose to ignore me and continued eating his sandwich. I climbed out of the van and approached him, feeling the beginnings of anger.

"Good afternoon . . . SSPCA," I said. "We had a call about a dead swan."

"News to me, son," said the guard with his mouth full, spitting ham on some paperwork.

Tripoli – lucky to be alive.

High voltage overhead wires are a death trap to such a large bird as a swan. In foggy weather swans fly straight into them and if they are not killed instantly they fall injured to the ground.

There was an embarrassing silence as he took another bite. For a second I wondered who had made the sandwich since it appeared to have been put together with loving care and I doubted very much that it was made by him. I could not help feeling that whoever lavished that attention on him was wasting their time. "Who called you, anyway?" he asked, sensing my annoyance and obviously determined to give me a hard time.

"You tell me." I said. "A Mr Gray, I think. This is the Longannet Power Station, isn't it?"

He picked up a radio and asked to speak to Mr Gray. "Aye, Mr Gray, gate security here, I have a lad fae the SPCA here, says they were called about a dead animal on the premises." He nodded in response, picking bits of sandwich from between his teeth. "Down near the ponds . . . right, I'll see to it." He put the radio down. "It's somewhere down near the ponds, been there all day apparently. Far side of the complex, near the pylons. Follow the main road to the main plant building, then left and left again."

I looked towards the complex and its two huge chimneys rising up into the mist from a tangled bed of concrete, pipe and pylon. I was instantly disheartened, knowing that if the swan had been lying in the same place all day it was almost certainly dead. I shuddered and wondered if my visit to this awful place was indeed worthless.

I was sure I would get lost but did not want to ask for clearer directions from the hostile security guard. I'd left the van's engine running and its purring as the barriers rose felt almost reassuring.

I tried to find my way around using the two huge chimneys looming large above me as points of reference, but I was lost. I drove in frustration until I spotted a small group of workers gathered outside a door.

One worker, an older man, glanced at me with what seemed like menace before taking a drag on his cigarette and turning his back to talk to someone else. A lad stood with his hands in his overall pockets kicking a plastic cup against the wall. He looked up for a second as I approached then returned to his game, spitting at the cup with accuracy and a look of defiance. It was the end of a long winter so I was already feeling depressed, and the atmosphere of this place certainly didn't help. In the mood I was in these men looked to me like creatures locked in a version of hell on earth.

I thought better of asking them for directions and put my foot down on the accelerator, keeping my eyes directly ahead. Thankfully I didn't have to turn around and eat humble pie, because almost immediately I spotted a sign to the holding ponds and breathed a sigh of relief.

Relief plummeted once again into despair as I spotted a large motionless white mass on an island of brown grass a short distance away. Against this

What I thought was a dead swan lay motionless on the grass, the purity of its white body starkly out of place.

dirty landscape its motionless, clean white body looked starkly out of place and it almost shone with purity. I didn't hurry since I had lost hope that it was still alive.

I looked up at the pylon wires lacing the sky like a spider's web. After physical impact with the wires and the ensuing electric shock the swan must have fallen at least 35 metres to the ground. Anyway, I knew that had it been alive it would have heard me coming and tried to move. A blast of wind flattened the grass and went straight through me, so cold and chilling it brought tears to my eyes. By the time I had blinked them away, I was kneeling next to the swan and could see that her eyes were still open and she was breathing. "You're alive," I whispered, feeling a sudden surge of excitement and a renewed sense of urgency.

She was a mute swan – mute by name only, because, of the three types of swans found in the United Kingdom, it is said to be the quietest. Protected by Royal grant in Britain, this was the species revered by kings and celebrated in music, art and poetry. How things had changed.

I saw by her beak that she was a female (males have a pronounced bulb on the beak and are generally larger, louder and less delicately built). I noticed she had a plastic band on one leg with the letters EEE inscribed – they seemed strangely familiar, perhaps she was one of ours?

She flinched only slightly as I gently manipulated her wings, and didn't even struggle when I gathered her up in my arms and walked back towards

These majestic birds were for me a graphic symbol of the head-on collision between wildlife and technology.

the van. A mute swan is a large bird, weighing from 8 to 16 kilograms and with a wing span of up to 1.5 metres. "Come on, let's get the hell out of here," I said, as another gust of wind cut through us.

The purring engine and the warmth of the van was familiar and comforting, to me at least, as I tried to make her as comfortable as I could on a hessian sack in the back. She offered no opposition and could barely lift her head. She just stared. I had seen birds this deep in shock before and already the prognosis was not good.

Ignoring the speed limit I traced my way back through the complex as best I could. One of the same group of workers noticed my speed and gesticulated his disapproval, encouraging others to let fly a rain of abuse.

"You too," I muttered angrily. The words I used were in fact less polite, but the meaning was the same.

I passed the security guard unnoticed, or more probably ignored, as he sat reading his paper, and was glad to get back onto the main road. The

In the mirror of the van I kept glancing at a bird I felt sure was close to death.

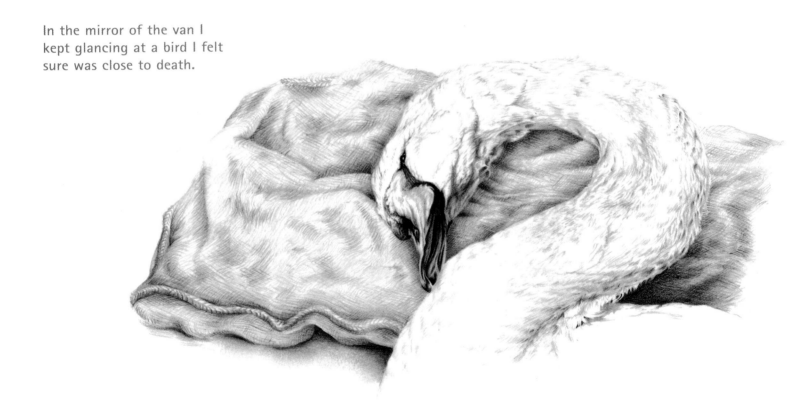

swan lay spread on the blanket, her head resting on a rubber boot. Her eyes were more tired and distant now and her breathing heavy and laboured, signs that she was fast nearing the end. I hurried towards the centre. I'd seen too many casualties caused by high voltage wires, and for me they were a graphic symbol of the head-on collision between wildlife and technology. The losers, it always seemed, were the creatures. And yet, if the creatures lost then we were all losers in the final analysis. It was not a good day for introspection, but as I drove I went over in my mind just how the accident may have happened . . . .

For the first time that day the sun reached out from behind the clouds and glowed orange across the mud flats of Torry Bay. Flocks of wading birds, busily feeding, fussed about in uneasy awareness of the dying light and the approach of an incoming tide. Now, lost in long shadows, they gathered together before taking flight. Even the echo of their calling faded without trace. By the water's edge, standing on huge webbed feet, a mute swan had raised its head, alert to their calls. For a moment longer it resumed tugging underwater at the eel grass it was feeding on, then dabbled the grass free of mud before swallowing and raising its head to look across the estuary again. Sensing the dying light, it waded into the water to take flight. Turning into the breeze, it lunged forward and opened its huge wings. With one enormous flap its wing tips cracked the water, and the symphony of its flight began.

Its webbed feet beat the surface of the water like a drum roll, gathering momentum before the steady rhythm of its wings took over. The swan became airborne and gradually gathered speed. It flew steadily and low up the estuary before gradually altering course inland. Its destination was a small loch that was its territory, a summer roosting and breeding place where its mate would perhaps be waiting.

As the water gave way to land, the swan's large white body was outlined against the concrete mass and black silhouettes of the power station and the tangle of intersecting pylons and cables. With its vision failing in the dusk, and unaware of the danger, the swan rose higher, putting itself unknowingly onto a collision course.

By the time it saw the cables it was too late. It made a frantic attempt to change direction, but its body and wings were too huge to slow down quickly enough and slammed hard into the cables. With a crack it catapulted through the air before thudding to the ground.

In hundreds of households the lights momentarily flickered . . . .

At Middlebank, I carried the almost unconscious swan indoors and placed her under a heat lamp. Gently I manipulated each wing to feel for breaks. A large purple area of bruising and burnt skin on the underside of one wing confirmed she had indeed hit the cable hard, but I could neither feel nor hear any breaks. With so much swelling it would be hard to tell without an x-ray.

Anxious to keep her alive I gave her fluids through a stomach tube and an injection to alleviate the shock. The fact that she was so weak and unable even to sit up was alarming, but there was nothing more I could do that night so I left her in peace. By the look in her eyes and her external injuries, I did not hold out much hope that she would see the dawn.

"Triple E," I thought, "Tripoli – that shall be your name then," and I entered her arrival and details in the record book. Then I searched back over our identification records. "I thought it was familiar," I muttered as I found the reference to EEE. She had in fact been reared at Middlebank three years previously, in 1988. She was one of four cygnets brought to the centre after being found covered with oil on the Forth/Clyde Canal. Two had died, but Tripoli was one of the survivors and, after being successfully cleaned, she had remained with us until able to fly and mature enough to be released.

Swans are generally fitted with two leg bands. One is small, made of metal and fairly inconspicuous with a personal number engraved on it. The other is deliberately large and marked clearly with letters that can be read from a distance without re-catching the bird.

Tripoli was one of our own birds, one of four oiled cygnets cleaned and reared at Middlebank three years earlier.

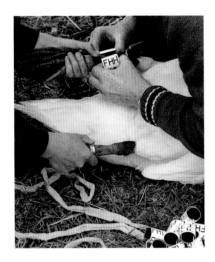

Allan and Lyndesay Brown ringed almost all of the swans that passed through Middlebank. This was part of a nationwide survey to keep track of their population and movements.

I noticed that I had in fact released her in the early autumn of that same year on Loch Leven, a nature reserve right in the middle of Fife about 30 kilometres away. Anxious to find out if there had been further sightings after that, I contacted Allan and Lyndesay Brown of the Lothian and Fife Swan Study Group – the couple who banded and kept track of Middlebank's swans.

The plot thickened. Allan told me that mute swan EEE had been seen several times around the Loch Leven area for some months after release. Then, some time later, it was sighted again at several lochs around Fife before it settled with a mate at Balbeggie Loch, only 27 kilometres from the centre. The pair had bred there successfully the previous summer, raising three cygnets to full maturity.

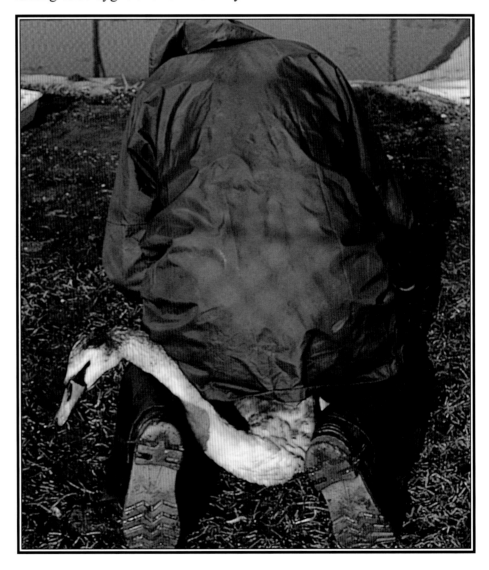

I looked out the window, cursing the darkness which descended so early in the depths of winter. Perhaps her mate was out there waiting for her return? I felt uneasy, knowing full well that swans mate for life and separation is an acute anxiety for them, even life-threatening. We cared for swans at Middlebank all the time, not just mute swans – the ones with the orange beaks most often seen around places occupied by human beings – but also occasionally the much wilder and wonderful subarctic sub-species called whooper swans, which fly down from Greenland and Iceland to winter over in Britain, and the smaller, rarer bewick swan.

I knew only too well what emotional and sensitive creatures swans were. They were big softies really. We'd had a pair of oiled swans flown in from Ulster for cleaning, and they had cried so much about separation we'd had to work on them together in the wash room. Swans, I knew, will go into a form of depression if separated, and I had seen them quite literally pine to death. They had equally strong instincts to protect their families and territory. The male could be as frightening as hell, and passionate in defending mate and offspring.

All of a sudden Tripoli's story was more personal than the crash between nature and technology; it was a story of love and separation. My first task the following day as I drove to work would be to check Balbeggie Loch for her mate. At dawn, when I focused my binoculars on Balbeggie Loch, I spotted very little except the sparkle of the sunrise on the water and the shapes of two dabbling ducks. There was, to my relief, no lone male mute swan, no mate waiting for the bird which I was almost sure would have died overnight.

Waiting would not only have been painful and worthless for the swan, but, in the absence of communication and the ability to explain, rather painful for us to watch. And yet I doubted that the male had already separated from his mate. By far the majority of swans remain together naturally, although they do occasionally divorce or have affairs. They certainly separate for days at a time, but they are only locally mobile, not migratory, and travel no more than a 40-kilometre radius, pairing up again in March or April to spend the summer together nesting and breeding.

Perhaps the mate too had been grounded or killed by pylon wires, I wondered. Perhaps he had fallen victim to the other common swan killers we dealt with so often – fishing tackle or oil, or lead poisoning from stray gunshot pellets and fishing sinkers which sit in sediment and are swallowed by dabbling birds? Even more likely, perhaps he had not yet arrived to secure the territory for summer, or was simply away feeding elsewhere.

I climbed back into the van and set off for work, wondering if the love

Perhaps her lifetime mate was out there pining, waiting for her return.

Opposite: Male mute swans such as this one have a more pronounced bulb on the beak and are generally larger, louder and less delicately built than females.

story would end the moment I looked into the centre's reception room at a dead female swan. To my surprise and joy she was still alive, but only just. She was very weak and unable to raise her head. For a creature that maintains such a graceful posture on land, water and in the air, it was disheartening to see her lying so awkwardly. And, knowing how fastidiously clean swans are, it was awful to see her pristine white plumage so soiled.

She squeaked weakly in protest when I force fed her more fluids. I felt a deep determination to try my best to promote this love story's happy ending.

By mid-morning we had secured an appointment with the vet to have Tripoli x-rayed. Not for the first time I cursed the fact the centre did not have the financial resources for its own x-ray equipment on site, and the fact that I was not qualified to use one even if we had. Placing our very sick swan back into the van and transporting it all the way to town and back seemed somehow to be defeating our purpose, but it had to be done. After several x-rays we put the images of Tripoli's skeleton against the light box and looked for any breaks. Miraculously, it confirmed that there were none.

Her wing bones, although very badly bruised, were still intact, and we were encouraged and hopeful that, provided the electrical burns around the

wound healed and there were no other complications, she would live. Her inability to raise her head and stand up was not, as I expected, caused by damage to her spine but was most probably a result of general shock. So, having acquired antibiotics and cream for her wounds, I left feeling quite hopeful. Tripoli's successful attempt to lift her head momentarily and look out of the rear windows of the van suggested we might just be winning.

After a week recuperating in a swan pen in the barn, where she lay on a soft, insulated plastic calf mat under a heat lamp, Tripoli was much improved. Although she had lost much of the burnt skin around the impact site, the swelling was subsiding and she was beginning to move her wing. She had also begun eating whole grain mix soaked in water and had started once again to resume the dignified, graceful posture that so typifies a swan.

With Tripoli now stabilised my mind turned once again to her mate. I decided another trip to Balbeggie Loch was in order, to try once again to capture the scattered pages of the love story. This time I was caught in a torrential downpour and I sat sheltered in the van looking through busy windscreen wipers across Balbeggie Loch, trying to make out a large white bird. He did not take long to spot. I raised my binoculars and struggled to get a clear view of him at the far end of the loch. With his head drooping, feathers puffed up and the raindrops like tears all around him, he was the picture of unhappiness. I could almost feel his despair and longing as he sat on the remains of the previous year's nest site. I recalled the despair in separation and the joy of reunion seen in adult swan pairs we'd had previously in the centre and I felt a little helpless.

"She's okay, she's okay," I found myself muttering, feeling despair at my inability to communicate the fact. I, too, was recovering from an unhappy love affair and broken heart, which contributed to my low spirits, and the plight of the lone male was like a mirror to my own suffering.

For a moment I played with the idea of at least letting him see his mate, perhaps from the shore, but dismissed the possibility, since it would only result in more stress for her, unable to escape us, and him, torn between fear of us and the desire to join her. In the past we had sometimes brought both mates in if one was injured, because we knew how distressed they became if separated. But even if it were easy to catch him, it was probably far too stressful an operation for all concerned.

His only solution was to be patient and wait for Tripoli to heal. But patience was a human quality. We could not know how far he would take his pining and how long he was willing to wait before perhaps leaving the breeding site and Tripoli. She and her mate were young, and although he was depressed at the present time it was still possible that he would move

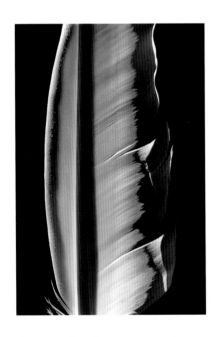
A swan feather – nature's perfect instrument of flight.

on in the weeks it would take Tripoli to recover. With her period of recuperation, the love story began a new and crucial chapter that would tell all about love being put to the test.

While Tripoli slowly recovered her mate waited and waited. After two more weeks he was causing us considerable concern since, despite our attempts with white, brown, toast or sandwich bread, he was very reluctant to feed and losing condition quickly. All we seemed to be achieving was the unwelcome establishment of a free-for-all feeding station on the Balbeggie farm estate, much to its owner's disapproval. There was clearly no question of the male swan's love and loyalty to Tripoli.

The next chapter began not a day too soon for us, when the vet gave Tripoli the green light for go. After five long weeks we could at last release and reunite her with her mate on the waters of Balbeggie Loch. It was a clear calm Sunday afternoon when Sandra Hogben and I, with great ceremony and watched by a small group of our regular volunteers, captured Tripoli in the swan enclosure and placed her carefully in a hessian sack for the journey. Although she looked uncomfortable with her head poking out one corner and the bottom tied up like a parcel, this was done to prevent her damaging herself trying to escape.

For the entire journey Tripoli looked eagerly out of the van window, perhaps perplexed at her direction. I sincerely hoped this would be her first and last experience of travelling backwards. From her occasional grunts and frequent peeping sounds it was clear she was eager to get out of her sack and the van and back to freedom.

At Balbeggie we were plunged into disappointment, for at first glance there appeared to be no mate swan. I confirmed this after a desperate and diligent scan of the loch and surrounding countryside with my binoculars.

For a while we pondered on the dilemma. Then, after much deliberation and continued searching, we decided to release Tripoli alone on the loch. At least she would be relatively safe there and we could continue to keep watch over her and supply additional food if necessary.

Our anticipated pleasure at her release, the kind of pleasure which brought to completion many of the Middlebank rescues, had been somewhat dampened. I took Tripoli from the back of the van. As soon as she sensed freedom she let out loud grunts and high-pitched squeaks and struggled wildly in the sack, while I strove to hold on. I placed sack and bird on the ground and began to undo the knot.

"Okay, okay, bonny lass, you're nearly there." I was finding the rope almost impossible to undo.

While I laboured with the knot, Tripoli continued struggling to escape and called out in anguish. Then, like a tap on my shoulder, the sudden echo

Swans, like geese, are best transported in sacks. This prevents damage caused by premature bids to escape.

of a swan's call in the distance caused me to look up. It was a higher pitched, piping, whistling sort of call, and I was hypnotised by the sight and sound of his return.

From far across the valley he gracefully descended to earth. Huge pure white wings stroked the air like pendulums, their sure, slow rhythmical beating a harmony of sight and sound. Transfixed, and in the silence such a moment demanded, we watched as he approached us to land. With an effortless glide he arced left then right and steadied himself just above the water, before bringing his huge webbed feet forward. As if on silk he glided across the surface, gradually letting it consume his weight, until he came to rest in a gentle surge of water. With a call of defiance, his eyes on Tripoli, he anxiously trod water.

Tripoli called and struggled even more, her mate called back, and I cursed as my awkward fingers tugged at the knot. At last it gave way. I loosened the hessian and, like a bar of soap from wet hands, Tripoli shot into the water with an explosive splash. Still on all fours I watched with joy as she swam straight towards her mate. With squeaks of welcome their reunion was sealed. Their heads were bowing to each other in union as they glided off towards the far end of the lake to preen and bathe away their experiences apart.

For a few moments I watched the ripples they made fade to calm in the distance. It was a fine chapter on which to end this love story, but it did not, of course, end the book. As far as I am aware Tripoli and her mate will live and love on for many summers upon the waters of Balbeggie Loch.

To me it is obvious why one of the most enduring great works of art is the love story and ballet called *Swan Lake*. We witnessed our own swan love story at Middlebank and were deeply touched by it. For me, though, swans are just one of the creatures who show us that love and devotion are not exclusively human qualities.

NOTES ON PHOTOGRAPHY

My FIRST CAMERA WAS DELIVERED BY SANTA ON CHRISTMAS DAY 1975, WHEN I WAS 10. THIS GREAT EVENT OCCURRED, I WAS TOLD, BECAUSE MY MOTHER HAD WRITTEN TO HIM IN DESPAIR AFTER THE FAMILY INSTAMATIC HAD GONE MISSING FOR THE UMPTEENTH TIME SOMEWHERE IN THE DEPTHS OF THE GARDEN OR MY BEDROOM. SOMEHOW, IT WAS ALWAYS ME THAT HAD IT LAST.

From then on, wherever I went my new camera went with me, usually in search of more creepy crawlies to record on film. Some of the photos scared my poor mother to death.

Serious photography began in earnest when I was able to save enough of my bookshop cleaning wages in 1979 to buy my first 35mm SLR (single lens reflex) camera. It was a very basic Russian job called a Zenith E, which was rugged to say the least. These cameras were built like tanks and looked as if they could withstand anything. That was certainly put to the test, withstanding more than one dip in the cold North Sea.

Nevertheless, it enabled me to learn the basics and to boast that I could capture something at one five-hundredth of a second. Modern SLR cameras can now achieve over four times that, but at 14 years of age with a rather light piggy bank I felt that one five-hundredth of a second was rather impressive.

Photography was an integral part of my course at art college, and I was then able to improve my equipment, knowledge and ability with more sophisticated 35mm SLRs, larger format cameras and a range of different films, both colour and black and white.

As a volunteer engrossed in the activities of the Middlebank animal rescue centre, sketching initially took precedence over photography. The cost of film was, as ever, a major constraint. I shifted my artistic focus back to photography from the time of the first oil spill in March 1987, when I began capturing events and casualties on film. While I was working at Middlebank there was very little time to sketch, but when there was an opportunity I photographed what I could. This habit became almost a part of daily life. If the sun was out, an interesting subject available, or some idea for an interesting shot pending, my camera was sure to be round my neck.

By then I had purchased my first Nikon camera body. Because of their high quality, Nikon equipment, and lenses in particular, are very expensive, so until 1990 I had to settle for a less expensive but effective Tamron 60–300mm lens. The camera body, the 301, was also at the lowest end of the Nikon range.

Most of my vast library of shots taken at Middlebank were shot with that one lens and camera body. My flash was very basic, one perhaps more suited to party snaps than wildlife, but it worked and gave results. This was very much a poor man's kit (such are the wages in wildlife rehabilitation), but I was able to prove to myself that quality results do not necessarily require expensive equipment. When I went to the Persian Gulf eco-disaster in 1991 I needed to upgrade my equipment, and, although it broke the bank, the purchase of Nikon 24mm and 105mm lenses proved invaluable. The 24mm continues to take the place of a standard 50mm lens.

In the Persian Gulf I had the opportunity to meet many top professional photographers working in the field. At times my limited equipment looked rather silly next to their huge camera bags, and for every shot I took they could afford to take five. I learned from them not to hold back on film but to use it as my prime resource. They taught me that although film is expensive it should always be used as if it is not. Easier said than done, but very true.

In 1992 I added a Nikon F3 to the 301, and a Benbo multi-functional tripod and a Metz flash system were also added to my still limited range of equipment.

I religiously use 35mm transparency film, most often Fuji Velvia or the faster Kodachrome 64 or 200 ASA. They both give me the quality results I look for.

I would describe myself as a non-technical, highly artistic photographer who relies much more on the eye than the camera. I am terrified of those auto-focus monsters and computer generated programs that do almost everything except make your toast in the morning. No doubt I will have to get used to these rapid developments, but I am more interested in what technology is doing to the environment and our attitudes towards it than I am in technology itself, and increasingly I find my images reflecting that.

I quietly worry that the day will arrive (if it has not already) when our children will much rather sit indoors exploring a computer program than explore the real world and the environment outside. The joys of collecting jars of frogs' spawn to watch metamorphose into tadpoles and of hunting in rock pools will slowly be lost, and with the loss of those experiences will disappear the wildlife itself and the respect we should be giving it. If we allow that to happen, we will certainly have lost our way.

Nature always has the last word.

John Stewart Collis (1900–1984)
Irish writer

ISBN 0 7336 0443 9

Contents © Darroch Donald 1996
A Hodder & Stoughton Book

First published in Australia 1996 by Hodder Headline Australia Pty Limited
(A member of the Hodder Headline Group)
10-16 South Street, Rydalmere, NSW 2116

Editorial Consultant: Kirsten Warner
Design: Trevor Newman
Production: Rochelle Renwick
Printed through Colorcraft, Hong Kong